PRAISE FOR *DESIGNING EXCEPTIONAL ORGANIZATIONAL CULTURES*

'As two experienced practitioners, Jamie Jacobs and Hema Crockett have unlocked the mysteries of organizational culture and provided a practical approach for learning and applying the important skills needed to drive an effective and sustainable culture. Their insights and examples are powerful. This book is an important read for all leaders invested in increasing engagement and motivation using values and belonging as tools.'
Dr Tony I Herrera, author of *Candor* and Senior Vice President of Executive Education and Development, LPL Financial

'Organizational culture is the most important factor for hiring and retaining high-performing talent and it's an area that so many organizations get wrong. This book clearly walks leaders through how to create a long-lasting culture that will out-perform your competition. A must read!'
Marshall Goldsmith, *New York Times* #1 bestselling author of *Triggers*, *Mojo* and *What Got You Here Won't Get You There*

'Culture eats everything for breakfast! That's the essential message from this book. Create a high-performing culture to achieve success on many levels: customer experience, employee experience and operational. It's a must-read for ambitious leaders seeking practical, detailed toolkits to create amazing organizations that competitors envy. As an executive coach, I love how the authors articulate the link between high-performing culture and the self-awareness of leaders. Every page oozes experience and expertise.'
Jacqui Harper MBE, Leadership Presence expert and author

'A company's future is dependent on nurturing its culture of today and what may be ahead. This book engages in the critical, thought-provoking topics that support unleashing the power of people. Designing a future in today's environment is more challenging than ever and the concepts explored in this book support creating an environment for high-performing teams to flourish.'
Linda Rogers, Senior Vice President, Human Resources, Dolby Laboratories

'I'm so excited for this book and the impact it will have on every leader who reads it, every organization they touch, and the lives of everyone involved. Culture is how we solve the most important problems, build the best companies, and enrich the lives of the most people. Kudos to Jamie Jacobs and Hema Crockett for their work and wisdom in writing it!'
Carey Ransom, Founder and President, Operate

'There are thousands of ways for teams to climb the metaphorical mountain of success. Yet, at the core, a well-developed culture that supports everyone's actions is paramount. Jamie Jacobs and Hema Crockett have done an exemplary job of simplifying and articulating how cultures can be intentionally created in this book. Having run multiple companies and worked with numerous cultures, this is a timely book for both aspiring and existing company executives.'
Tony Enrico, CEO and author of *Championship Selling*

'A must-read for every business and HR leader. Organizational culture is the most important factor for attracting and retaining high-performing talent and it's one area that many organizations get wrong. This book clearly walks leaders through how to create a long-lasting culture that will out-perform your competition. Especially valuable are the "Questions to Ask" at the end of the chapters, which serve to help the reader digest the content and reflect on how to apply their learnings within their own organization.'
Edie L Goldberg PhD, author, speaker and consultant, and co-author of *The Inside Gig*

Designing Exceptional Organizational Cultures

How to develop companies where employees thrive

Jamie Jacobs
Hema Crockett

Publisher's note

Every possible effort has been made to ensure that the information contained in this book is accurate at the time of going to press, and the publishers and authors cannot accept responsibility for any errors or omissions, however caused. No responsibility for loss or damage occasioned to any person acting, or refraining from action, as a result of the material in this publication can be accepted by the editor, the publisher or the authors.

First published in Great Britain and the United States in 2021 by Kogan Page Limited

Apart from any fair dealing for the purposes of research or private study, or criticism or review, as permitted under the Copyright, Designs and Patents Act 1988, this publication may only be reproduced, stored or transmitted, in any form or by any means, with the prior permission in writing of the publishers, or in the case of reprographic reproduction in accordance with the terms and licences issued by the CLA. Enquiries concerning reproduction outside these terms should be sent to the publishers at the undermentioned addresses:

2nd Floor, 45 Gee Street	122 W 27th St, 10th Floor	4737/23 Ansari Road
London	New York, NY 10001	Daryaganj
EC1V 3RS	USA	New Delhi 110002
United Kingdom		India

www.koganpage.com

Kogan Page books are printed on paper from sustainable forests.

© Jamie Jacobs and Hema Crockett, 2021

The right of Jamie Jacobs and Hema Crockett to be identified as the authors of this work has been asserted by them in accordance with the Copyright, Designs and Patents Act 1988.

ISBNs

Hardback   978 1 78966 723 3
Paperback   978 1 78966 721 9
Ebook   978 1 78966 722 6

British Library Cataloguing-in-Publication Data

A CIP record for this book is available from the British Library.

Library of Congress Cataloging-in-Publication Data

Names: Jacobs, Jamie Latiano, author. | Crockett, Hema, author.
Title: Designing exceptional organizational cultures : how to develop
   companies where employees thrive / Jamie Jacobs, Hema Crockett.
Description: London ; New York, NY : Kogan Page, 2021. | Includes
   bibliographical references and index.
Identifiers: LCCN 2020050342 (print) | LCCN 2020050343 (ebook) | ISBN
   9781789667219 (paperback) | ISBN 9781789667233 (hardback) | ISBN
   9781789667226 (ebook)
Subjects: LCSH: Corporate culture. | Organizational behavior. | Personnel
   management. | Performance.
Classification: LCC HD58.7 .J339 2021 (print) | LCC HD58.7 (ebook) | DDC
   658.3–dc23
LC record available at https://lccn.loc.gov/2020050342
LC ebook record available at https://lccn.loc.gov/2020050343

Typeset by Integra Software Services, Pondicherry
Print production managed by Jellyfish
Printed and bound by CPI Group (UK) Ltd, Croydon CR0 4YY

CONTENTS

List of figures ix
About the authors x
Foreword xi
Acknowledgements xiv

Introduction: C is for conscious 1

01 What is organizational culture? 9
What is culture anyway? 10
The biggest challenges you face 18
Common pitfalls 21
Questions to ask 22
Moving to action: what you can do next 23
Lessons from the real world 24
Final thoughts 25

02 Why top-performing cultures don't happen by accident 27
Culture is a feedback loop 29
The role of leadership in culture 30
Building self-awareness 32
Establishing a baseline 35
The toxic culture lifecycle of a non-self-aware leader 38
The high-performing culture lifecycle of a self-aware leader 40
People are watching 41
Common pitfalls 42
Questions to ask 44
Moving to action: what you can do next 45
Lessons from the real world 48
Final thoughts 49
Endnotes 49

03 Organizational structure 51

Types of organizational structures 52
What's structure got to do with culture? 54
If you build it, they will come 56
Redefine your project 59
A new kind of team 61
Leadership expectations and structure 64
Whose job is it anyway? 65
Burnout 67
Common pitfalls 68
Questions to ask 69
Moving to action: what you can do next 71
Lessons from the real world 72
Final thoughts 73
Endnote 74

04 Identifying and defining core values 75

What are core values? 75
Why are core values important? 76
Defining your values 78
Checking in with your values 86
Bringing your core values to life 88
Core values lead to core behaviour 92
Common pitfalls 94
Questions to ask 96
Moving to action: what you can do next 97
Lessons from the real world 98
Final thoughts 99
Endnotes 99

05 Skills for now and the future 101

Natural born leaders? 109
Customizing competencies 111
Consistency is key 113
Infusing core competencies 113
Core competencies revisited 114

Welcome to the dark side 115
Common pitfalls 116
Questions to ask 117
Moving to action: what you can do next 118
Lessons from the real world 119
Final thoughts 122
Endnotes 123

06 Attracting and retaining the right talent 125

Why should someone work for your organization? 126
Using the EVP to attract the right talent 134
Opting out is okay 135
A values fit is more important than a culture fit 137
But what about the values questions? 138
Recruiting leaders 140
Common pitfalls 140
Questions to ask 143
Moving to action: what you can do next 143
Lessons from the real world 144
Final thoughts 146
Endnotes 146

07 Engagement and motivation 147

To do or not to do: engagement surveys? 149
Using surveys for good 151
Other sources of feedback 154
The simple art of listening 158
Connecting skills to each employee 159
Ideal state for engagement 162
Measurement through metrics 163
Common pitfalls 164
Questions to ask 165
Moving to action: what you can do next 166
Lessons from the real world 167
Final thoughts 168
Endnotes 168

08 Total Rewards 171

Components of TR 172
The role of TR in designing an exceptional organizational culture 174
Personalized rewards 176
What do your rewards say about your organization? 180
Beyond pay and benefits 184
Common pitfalls 186
Questions to ask 188
Moving to action: what you can do next 189
Lessons from the real world 190
Final thoughts 192
Endnotes 193

09 Diversity, inclusion, and belonging 195

DI&B is not a quota 196
Walk the talk 198
Measuring the ROI 199
Employer brand and diversity 203
So you have diverse leadership, now what? 204
Bringing it back to self-awareness 205
Common pitfalls 207
Questions to ask 208
Moving to action: what you can do next 209
Lessons from the real world 211
Final thoughts 212
Endnotes 213

10 Moving to action 215

The importance of change management 221
Final thoughts 224

Index 226

LIST OF FIGURES

FIGURES

Figure 1.1	The intersection of culture	12
Figure 3.1	Most commonly used structures	52
Figure 4.1	The Golden Circle Revisited as adapted from Simon Sinek's The Golden Circle (04 May 2010)	77
Figure 4.2	Core values best practices	82
Figure 4.3	Core values categories	83
Figure 4.4	The what and how of performance evaluations	90
Figure 6.1	Creating an EVP	129
Figure 8.1	CSR categories	185

ABOUT THE AUTHORS

Hema Crockett and Jamie Jacobs joined forces in 2018 to co-found High Performanceology, a management consulting firm that shows enterprising organizations how to build and sustain leadership cultures to cultivate and retain talent and produce optimum results. Synthesizing decades of combined experience as business and HR executives across a broad range of companies and industries, Hema and Jamie also provide their vast client base with esteemed reputations as coaches and HR community leaders. With a team of forward-thinking professionals specialized in talent and HR, High Performanceology can help transform any company's organizational infrastructure into 'a place people want to work'.

Hema and Jamie also founded Gig Talent, a modern talent agency that has cultivated a vibrant community of first-class HR consultants and coaches and created the first HR Consulting Certification Programme, which sets the standard for HR consultants and coaches.

FOREWORD

Before I talk about Hema Crockett and Jamie Jacobs' latest book, *Designing Exceptional Organizational Cultures*, let me talk about values and culture in general.

When I was given the privilege to lead as CEO of WD-40 Company nearly 23 years ago I realized that we needed to undergo a cultural transformation. We needed to break down the silos of knowledge and transform them into fields of learning. We needed to create a learning culture, one in which there were no failures at all, only learning moments. What we needed was a culture built on people. Seeking inspiration from the Aboriginal tribes of Australia I discovered the bonds and attributes of a tribal culture. Attributes such as knowledge, celebration, a strong sense of belonging and, above all else, values.

As Hema and Jamie convey right at the onset, culture starts with the self-awareness of leaders and our ability to take a close look at our own values and behaviours. If there is misalignment, the repercussions can be felt throughout the organization, undermining the culture. Perhaps one of the most important points that resonates so closely with me and the work we do at WD-40 Company is the fact that culture is intentional. It doesn't just happen by accident. As mentioned, I started on this journey to transform the WD-40 Company culture over 20 years ago. Since we started, not a day goes by that we don't tinker or tweak or review some aspect of our culture to ensure it is still meeting our needs and the needs of our customers. We have been intentional, and like Hema and Jamie state, 'In businesses where culture is paramount and made into a business priority (or even a goal or objective), it becomes everyone's priority'. Culture is our priority at WD-40 Company.

In order to create a tribal culture at WD-40 Company, we needed to start with our organizational values. I greatly believe that values have always been the foundation upon which any culture is built and, as Hema and Jamie outline in Chapter 4, identifying and defining core values help build the framework by which all other decisions are made. The WD-40 Company values are:

- We value creating positive, lasting memories in all our relationships.
- We value making it better than it is today.
- We value succeeding as a tribe while excelling as individuals.
- We value owning it and passionately acting on it.
- We value sustaining the WD-40 Company economy.

Often leaders forget that values need to be meaningful. They aren't just words written on a wall, but they are woven into the fabric of the culture; they are part of every layer. Our values, in conjunction with our four pillars of Care, Candour, Accountability and Responsibility became the basis of our new culture. I deeply appreciate Hema and Jamie's ability to use values as a guide throughout *Designing Exceptional Organizational Cultures*. They have beautifully connected the criticality of values with how you pay employees, how you engage them, how you build trust and loyalty. Hema and Jamie present an invaluable guide on how organizations can intentionally build a culture that not only results in high engagement but in business results as well. What they present is timeless, relevant and practical.

For us, our values and culture have helped create an amazing tribe of individuals who come together as one united team. As a tribe, we've created a culture in which each tribe member is considered a leader, a developer of people, whether themselves or others. Each is also an important contributor to the business. The people, our tribe, is what makes us successful.

Our progress can be measured in multiple ways. Our March 2020 global engagement survey saw a 95 per cent completion rate and showed an overall engagement of 93 per cent. Among our highest scoring items, at 97.5 per cent, was 'I feel my opinion and values are a good fit with WD-40 Company culture'. While these numbers are great, they only tell half the story. Our financial success is further proof of the importance of a strong and thriving culture. In the 20 plus years we have committed ourselves to a learning culture built on a solid foundation of values, we have seen our sales quadruple. Our market cap increased from $250 million to nearly $2.5 billion in that time.

I love the progress we've made, the stories we've shared, the success we've experienced as a tribe. I know the importance of a thriving culture. And I know cultivating a healthy and long-lasting culture is a journey. The work is never done. This is why I am delighted to be writing the Foreword to this book.

My hope is that you enjoy it as much as I have. Even if you have an amazing culture today, I guarantee you will pick up something new when reading this. This book provides insights for any business and HR leaders who are looking to transform their organization by creating and cultivating an award-winning organizational culture. It also provides a roadmap or blueprint that, when followed, will get you the high-performing organization you are looking for. I am confident that, after reading this book, you will feel as energized as I am and be left with a deeper understanding of yourself as a leader, a clear definition of what culture looks like for your organization and the motivation and determination to go out and build it.

With that, I leave you to read and internalize *Designing Exceptional Organizational Cultures*.

And don't forget, the amazing product in the small blue and yellow can with the red top that can make a difference in your world if you need it.

G'day.

Garry Ridge
Chairman and CEO
WD-40 Company

ACKNOWLEDGEMENTS

First and foremost, we would like to thank our husbands, Michael Crockett and Josh Jacobs, for supporting us in this endeavour. We love you both! We would also like to thank our families for their encouragement as we took this on. To our dear friends and colleagues from whom we've learned throughout the years and were kind enough to contribute their insights, thank you for taking the time to contribute. A special thank you to Rea Frey, who has been with us on this journey for nearly two years now. Thank you for guiding us and steering us when we needed it the most. And last, but not least, thank you to Lucy Carter, Anne-Marie Heeney and everyone on the Kogan Page team for allowing us to be part of the Kogan Page family.

Introduction: C is for conscious

Hema: As I stood at the base of Everest, I knew I had done what many dream of doing. I was out of my comfort zone and loving it. I stared up at a scoop of white meringue in a shot of blue sky. This trek had claimed so many. As I gauged the daunting peak, my lungs grappled for breath.

This was day six of the trek to get to Base Camp. We started out around 6:30 am, our usual time, from the tea house. Our guide, my friend Kevin, and I navigated the five and a half hours between the tea house and Base Camp. With each blind curve around the steep cliffs, Everest was coming clearly into view. It was a bright sunny day and the top of the world awaited.

As I approached, I was not really thinking about what my body had done. I was just ready to see it. And then there we were – nearly 18,000 feet of altitude eaten away. The air ripped through my body, cleaner than any before it. I was in awe of the views, the mass of Everest, and a bit blinded as the sun bore down on the white untouched snow. I thought of my husband, Mike, and how proud he would be.

As Kevin and I took pictures and talked to those who were living at Base Camp, it hit me: *I'd done it*. Up at nearly 18,000 feet, the wind screamed, my body was a little sore, and yet I felt more alive in that single moment than all the thousands before. I wasn't lost in distractions, deadlines, meetings, or the senseless daily tasks that compose so many of our lives. Instead, I stood rooted on that mountain and realized that not only had I conquered Base Camp – I had finally conquered my mind.

Without overthinking anything and without giving up; hell, even without a shower. That luxury would come around day eight.

Before Everest, I had a high-paying corporate position as an account executive for a large, well-respected brokerage firm, and an office with a view. I was leading a team, doing the work I was good at, and helping clients and industries who were changing the world. My team was considered high performing, so that is exactly what we were going to be. At all costs. I worked early mornings, late into the night, and even on weekends. I worked the day before my wedding. The day after my wedding. Even from a hospital bed while in the ER (#truestory). I thought I was happy and fulfilled.

Then came the call.

'Hema, we're moving to Nepal.' My husband delivered the news while I was knee-deep in meetings. Mike was being transferred on a special assignment to work with the US State Department. It was a great opportunity for him and a chance for us to see the world. In all my plans, travel was a huge personal goal, but somewhere along the way, on the climb up the corporate ladder, I had got stuck and forgotten to go.

As I walked into my boss's office to break the news, I did not know how to feel. I was excited for an adventure but terrified of losing my identity – an identity that was tied directly to my work. I had a psychological allegiance to my work. I defended it. I protected it. I would do *anything* for it.

The day I delivered the news, I wavered between my loyalty to the job and my yearning to see a world I worked so hard to live in. But with all the late nights and sacrifices, was I really living? Was I out in the world, or up here in a cushy office? When had I stopped taking risks?

When I walked out of the office that day, I decided I was willing to try on another identity. It was time.

Just a few short months later, we arrived in Kathmandu at 11 pm. The darkness was absolute. As our eyes adjusted to the inky night, I saw piles of trash lining the road.

'Trash strike,' our driver explained.

I glimpsed the intimate, discarded lining of people's lives as we bumped along the street in our armoured vehicle, past curfew (the privilege of diplomatic plates), in a country so exotic, most people hadn't even visited. As I turned to my husband, flashes of my old life gripped me around the throat. Suddenly, I missed my safe routine, the predictability of the office, our warm, familiar bed. As I searched for his face in the opaque space between us, the only thought I had was, 'Why did you bring me here?'

Silently, we drove onto the compound that would become home for the foreseeable future. Large gates swung open to reveal a seven-foot wall with three feet of anti-climb wire, surrounding a three-storey house with bars on every window.

'Welcome home,' Mike whispered.

It did not feel like home. It did not look like home. I *missed* home. But I had agreed to this adventure. As we unloaded our bags and stepped inside, I made a promise to myself: *I would try*. That was all I could really do.

Fast forward four weeks (after the jet lag faded and I acclimatized to the altitude), and Kathmandu did feel like home. The US Embassy where Mike worked was only a short walk away, and I got to know many of the other Americans very quickly. They had been through the same circumstances when they first landed in Kathmandu, so listening to their stories helped. We would go on outings to various temples, places of interest, markets, and bazaars. The sights, the sounds, and the smells were like nothing I had ever experienced (and like nothing I have experienced since). The people were friendly, caring, and ready to engage in real conversations. There was no hustle here.

Despite getting comfortable in my environment, not having a job was new for me, so my goal became to find one. Luckily, I was hired by the State Department and subsequently the Department of Justice. I didn't have my office with a view, and I was no longer leading a team, but my relationship to work was starting to change. It was not about a job. It was about purpose and meaningful work, a feeling that I *thought* I had before, but nothing compared to this. When I was at work, I was happy. There were not the same intense pressures of meeting impossible deadlines and living in a culture where hectic was the normal pace. Here, I was patient and fully engaged. And when I left work for the day, *I left work for the day*.

After my epic two-week trek to Base Camp, we left Nepal after nearly 18 months. However, I did not leave Nepal the same person who arrived. I didn't know it at the time, but Nepal profoundly changed the way I viewed people, my relationship to work, and most importantly, my relationship to myself.

In the spring of 2013, after a stint in Berlin, my husband and I returned to the United States. We had been gone for three years, and I was terrified. Not of reentering my home, but of reverting right back to my old habits and getting sucked in (or is it suckered?) to leading a team, using people as a means to an end, driving high performance regardless of the impact, and never being able to truly step away and shut down.

All of my gifts of connecting, disconnecting, and reconnecting seemed to waver outside of the Nepalese environment. If I did not change my environment, then how was I supposed to change my relationship to it?

I knew I could not return to my old habits. It was no way to live. I was determined not to go down the same road again. I realized what made my relationship to work in Nepal so profound was the *meaning* behind it. It was not just about meeting deadlines or collecting a paycheck – I had *purpose*.

Despite that reverie, nearly seven years after leaving Nepal, I found myself right back in that corner office leading a high-performing team, meeting deadlines, working 65+ hours per week, and lacking balance. It was a cycle, one many of us are all too familiar with. So, it was time to make a decision – continue receiving a paycheck, hating every moment of every day and wishing I was doing anything else, or make the leap for a true and long-lasting change. I chose to change and strike that balance every moment of every day.

As I reflected on my time in Nepal and the years after, what I'd brought home with me was a journey of self-discovery and recalibration; a realization that being high performing doesn't mean you are always 'on', but rather striking a balance between working hard and stepping away to recharge. In our hyper-connected world, I knew that it was going to be hard.

But, if I wanted to find that balance, that alignment that allowed me to be high performing and innovative, I had to dig deep and understand what I wanted my relationship to be with my co-workers, peers, and those who reported to me. And most of all, I realized that the employer/employee relationship is a two-way street: if organizations want to succeed in the future and achieve sustainable business results, then they need to be places where people want to work. They need to create environments where people are committed to achieving excellence and high performance. They need to construct systems where HR and executives walk the talk; where there are shared values and goals.

This journey eventually led to the creation of High Performanceology and our work's mission to create organizations where people thrive and grow. Now I am on a mission to take all I have learned and apply it here, for *you*. No, you do not have to move to another country to have the same monumental transformation. You can achieve happiness and balance in your workplace, today. You can attract and maintain the right talent now. You can 'have it all,' but in ways that really matter.

Jamie: Like Hema, I had my own struggle with work (though I did not get to explore another country to come to this startling revelation). My metamorphosis was more subtle, but one day, I remember standing in my large corner office, staring out the window. Behind me, I had everything I had ever wanted. I was a senior director with a global Fortune 50 organization. I had worked my way up to running talent acquisition and HR business partnership across the United States and Canada, leading enterprise-level transformations and optimizations, and I was also the local President of the National Human Resources Organization. By the age of 32, I, Jamie Jacobs, was 'going places'.

Despite these accomplishments, I felt oddly disconnected from it all. What I thought I had been searching for at work and in my personal life suddenly wasn't enough. What I was searching for I could not find in an office (or so I thought).

For me, this was the start of a very personal journey. After floundering in my mind for a few months, I sought out a coach and began to understand that fear was playing a subconscious, yet significant, role in my life. Being high performing and recognized by external validation was missing the connection to my own personal values about what was important. I worked to identify my own vision of what I wanted from both my personal and professional life, not limiting it to what I could imagine at the time. This energy and focus shift had a significant impact on how I showed up both at work and at home. The recognition that everything is a choice was incredibly empowering.

With my coach's support, I literally created powerful vision statements about my desired state, let go of what was not serving me, and became much more intentional with my time and purpose. In hindsight, this was more of an incremental adjustment and really more about alignment, but at the time, it felt life changing.

Instead of being a leader driven by growing within whatever system I happened to be playing in, I began to become a leader who had my own set of values and beliefs. I saw the transformation that this made for me personally and could see the increased impact I had with others.

As I got clear, I had an increased ability to coach, lead, and inspire others and ultimately drive impact at both a personal and department level. The 'why' in my professional motivation became this: *as leaders and organizations, we have an obligation to create places where people can develop, grow, and thrive at work.* Helping others lean into their individual power by aligning within themselves is the most gratifying work I have done. Life is short, we have many choices, and we do not need to be subject to the systems or expectations around us. As leaders, we have an obligation to take an active role in shaping these systems with an awareness of everyone within, including both employees and customers.

In order for that to happen, the HR and executive teams need to do their own personal work. This allows them the perspective to create a vision of a culture and work environment for high-performing, highly motivated teams to deliver excellence, have fun, and win in the marketplace. When Hema and I talked, she basically mirrored these exact feelings. Together, we created High Performanceology and made it our work's mission to create organizations where people thrive and grow.

What does that have to do with you? Maybe as a CEO, you are forward thinking and innovative. You know that in order to scale your organization, you need to do something different. You are just not sure *what*. Maybe as an HR leader, you know you need to lead the transformation hand-in-hand with your CEO to ensure your organization succeeds into the future. But where to begin? With all the books, podcasts, blogs, and opinions out there, it can be an overwhelming landscape to wade through.

Here's a fact we can all agree upon, however: today's work environment looks very different to that of our grandparents' or even parents' generation. Maybe these changes just occur with time. Maybe it's a generational thing. From the way we recruit (no more standing in line and getting hired the same day) to the way we communicate (slack versus written letters), nothing is the same. Hell, cubicles have given way to couches and co-working spaces. Don't get us wrong, we like this shift. We had an office in a co-working space that served us well and adjusted like many others with the 'work from anywhere' revolution to a completely remote team.

But if all of these things are changing the work environment, why do business leaders think treating people the same old way and doing the same old thing will make their organization successful? News flash: it won't.

Whether you decided to read this book because you have a motivation to prepare your personal leadership for the way work is changing, or you feel responsibility to prepare your organization at an enterprise level for this change, it is our intention to share actionable steps for you to take that will create impact in aligning both personal motivation and organizational purpose while developing operational processes and systems that will allow you to strategically adapt as things evolve and change, both internally and externally (yes, that is a long sentence).

What we have built here is a process of *intentionally* building organizational culture, because, in case you have not heard, culture is the single leading factor in a company's success – or failure. This isn't a one and done process. This is continuous and will allow you to adapt to the way work is changing and guide your organization, regardless of your title, through that change. But, we promise if you stick with this process, your organizational culture will look radically different than when you started.

It's all up to you.

01

What is organizational culture?

High-performing cultures where people are given autonomy to do their work, a clear path to succeed, and a common purpose to do amazing work... all out-perform their competition. Study after study has shown that great cultures get great results. They also get higher profits, if you want that sort of thing.

CHRIS DYER, PERFORMANCE CONSULTANT,
BESTSELLING AUTHOR AND CEO AT PEOPLEG2

What's your why?

We like to define your why as your purpose, which is where it all begins. Often people jump right into the 'what' (the journey) without first stopping to get clear about their own why and create stakeholder buy-in to bring people along with them on the journey. This buy-in starts with you and the leadership team. *Why* did you pick up this book? What do you hope to change or create?

If we had to guess, one reason is because you want to be successful as an individual leader and you want to build a high-performing organization that is well positioned for success into the future – so well positioned that your competitors are looking to you for advice and talent is knocking at your door to be part of your team. It may be that you have a sense of either an opportunity to make things even better than they are or a need to make some shifts to correct things that seem off track.

In this book, you will learn to work as a collective unit within your organization to create *one* roadmap – that's right, *one*. With your why in hand, you can start focusing on the 'what', or the actual journey. Discover ways to engage others on the journey regardless of what your starting point is. Together, you will be speaking the same language, driving to the same outcome, and holding each other accountable along the way.

What is culture anyway?

When you think about designing exceptional organizational culture, what comes to mind? Culture has become such a common word we toss around; a buzzword for reasons to join or leave an organization. Culture is much more meaningful than just a word, yet we often build culture as we go. We do not set the foundation or clear intention first because we don't have time. We hire and fire, we pivot, and we lose a lot of time and money in the process, not realizing that we are setting the culture unintentionally as we go.

Whether you have already built your ship and it is running (mostly) smoothly, or if it's time to reimagine your culture, looking through various lenses is going to be vital. We're going to suggest three different lenses to look at culture:

- yourself as leader;
- your team as example;
- your organization as a whole.

All three of these points are instrumental and interconnected. The organization does not exist without teams, and teams do not exist without you. Each of these components needs to be solid and aligned to ensure the ultimate outcome. Looking through these lenses will inform you as you determine your path to your desired organizational culture.

> **CULTURE QUOTE**
>
> My advice to business leaders is that culture is not a purely collective or organizational concept. It is a collection of specific multiple dimensions done well or poorly, and conscious choices and tradeoffs must be made to shape and prioritize cultural dimensions such as shared beliefs, norms, artifacts, who has power, how failure is handled, etc. Culture is also best understood and most powerful at the local team level, not at the broader companywide level, since that is where performance actually happens.
>
> *Ian Ziskin, President of EXec Excel Group LLC*

First, let's look at what organizational culture even means. And we promise, it is not as simple as ping pong tables, kegs in the breakroom, an inspirational quote posted on a wall, an employee handbook, or an idea defined by any one person. Then what is it? Our definition revolves around values and accepted behaviours that are demonstrated through everyone's actions. These are what drive a company's culture. *Culture* is demonstrated in the answer to the question, 'What's it really like to work there?' Without a reasonable definition, you cannot see the critical links to other key elements in an organization, like leadership, structure, decision making, and incentives.

While people might have their own definitions, the two elements people can agree on are that (1) it exists and (2) it plays a crucial role in shaping behaviours in an organization.

Your culture is what creates that special sauce that makes your organization unique; it's the DNA that makes you special and stand out from the rest; it's what makes you attractive (or unattractive, if you have a bad or unhealthy culture). Good culture doesn't happen by accident. Culture is formed by the interactions people have with one another. Culture is what happens when actions, behaviours, and values intersect, as seen in Figure 1.1. In other words, it is the ecosystem of any organization.

FIGURE 1.1 The intersection of culture

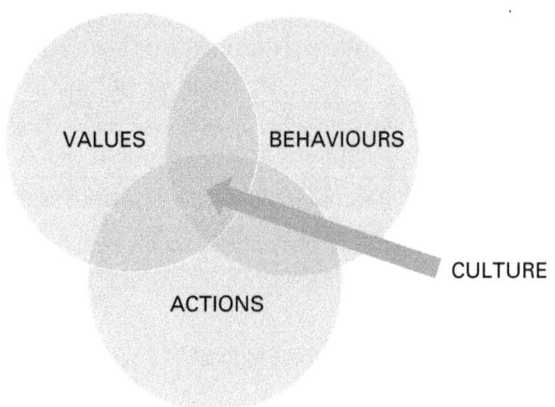

This intersection is influenced by leadership, team dynamics and incentives (what people are incentivized to do, whether monetarily or non-monetarily). In addition, the intersection of actions, behaviours and values helps define reality within a specific organization; a common set of jointly held beliefs and principles shared by all employees. These beliefs and principles are unique to each organization. Leaders and employees are the ones who give these beliefs and principles meaning and these meanings shift over time.

How culture is viewed can differ based on your lens, as we mentioned previously. Let's take a deeper dive into you, your team, and your organization as a whole.

Yourself as leader

Before you can get a handle on your team, organization, or products, you need to gain self-awareness of yourself as a leader. Because your culture starts with you.

We could share many stories about business failures (of which there are quite a few), leading organizational change (which we've built our careers on), or building rockstar teams (we have won awards for building amazing HR teams, just sayin'). However, we chose to start with something personal because without our personal 'aha' moments, we never would have created those award-winning teams and we would not have been able to lead our various organizations through change.

CASE STUDY

Early in her career, Jamie worked for a leader in a large, highly matrixed, global company. Her leader had dual reporting lines, one to a functional corporate leader and the other to a regional president. The dynamics between the two managing executives were contentious and made it extremely difficult to please both. The leader tried to please both of the other leaders, which was basically impossible. Jamie observed her go between them and as she went back and forth, she continued to lose the respect of each as she did not meet their expectations and failed to assert her own leadership point of view. Not long after, she was removed from that role and was eventually replaced with a new leader. This new leader came into the same situation but had a very different approach. She was very grounded in doing what she felt was right. She would make decisions and lead her team based on this and equally disregarded the agendas of her two bosses unless it was aligned with what was right for the business and the team. An example of how this showed up was that she would get up and leave a meeting if she felt that she did not need to be there. The value was time management and team empowerment; it wasn't that she was rude, but she protected her time and the time of others. She would make recommendations and business plans and tell her managers what the plan was for areas within her responsibility rather than trying to get them to agree on an approach. The way that each of these leaders responded to this situation could not have differed more and the results they achieved differed dramatically. One was clearly more effective than the other. Having the benefit of observing this lesson early allowed Jamie to contrast the difference between the two and try to integrate that into her own leadership style. Establishing your leadership values and integrating them into your leadership style and brand is critical to being an effective leader.

Taking an honest inventory of ourselves is a great place to start. Let's walk through a series of questions that will help you reflect on your current leadership effectiveness and leadership brand. Answer the following questions honestly for yourself:

1 As a leader, how do you currently show up? How would others describe you? (If you have trouble answering this one, consider asking some trusted colleagues for feedback.)

2 As a leader, how do you wish you showed up? (Hint here, reflect on the best leader you've had; what made them a strong leader?)
3 What prevents you from being this type of leader already?
4 Have you defined your own leadership values? Are you in alignment with them? Do others know what you are all about? How do you demonstrate them in your daily routine, actions, and behaviours?
5 Do you have a defined set of leadership principles you live by? Are you consistent? When are you not consistent?
6 What are your unique strengths as a leader?

In reflecting on your answers, is there a difference between how you show up and who you desire to be? Are there things that you can identify that are barriers to your effectiveness? This assessment will help you create a meaningful action plan for yourself.

With this information and reflection, take a moment to identify two or three actions you would like to commit to in order to improve your personal alignment with your leadership values and desired organizational culture. This dedicated energy that you are bringing to this self-assessment will no doubt make a significant difference in how you show up and connect with others. Imagine if all the leaders on your team demonstrated a similar commitment to self-reflection, growth, and impact.

> **CULTURE QUOTE**
>
> Figure out how to become self-aware – that will help you understand your strengths, your gaps and how others best complement you; embrace them and create an open-minded, diverse and inclusive team and an honest process for decision making that is rigorous and accessible. That will create a strong culture, where input is valued, candour is expected, and best team/company outcomes are preferred vs individual heroics. This culture will create a natural magnet to attract and retain the best talent.
>
> *Carey Ransom, Founder and President at Operate*

Team dynamics: set the example

You have already started to look at your own leadership reputation or brand; now we are looking at that of your team. The culture of your team is a result of what each of the members decides to bring to the team every single day. Keeping an accurate pulse on your team's culture and team effectiveness is part of your role as the leader.

Let's do a similar exercise to assess the current state of your team. When looking at your team, if you are honest, you may see a really healthy, high-performing team. You also might see a mix of strong performers and some who appear disengaged. You might even be hit with a reality of some dysfunction or poor performance that you have been avoiding or unaware of. The challenge here is to take a real inventory. We recognize that this can be difficult because at the end of the day you as the leader are responsible. It might even feel overwhelming. How do you eat an elephant? One bite at a time. What we can guarantee is that if you don't look at it, you might miss opportunities to keep the great things working great and opportunities to improve the things that aren't working. Again, answer these questions honestly:

- Is your team clear about the team and organization's vision?
- What is the current emotional state of your team? Consider this both through the lens of the collective team and also of each individual member of the team.
- What is the desired emotional state of your team?
- What does your team's body language say?
- How do you motivate your team?
- Do you know what drives each member of the team?
- How inclusive is your team? In meetings, is everyone's voice heard? Are there some people who stay quiet? Is there anyone that the team is working around or not including? If so, why?
- How does your team exhibit the organization's values? Do they consistently model them?
- What do other leaders say about your team?

- Do you know what each person's strengths are? Are they being leveraged within the team dynamics?
- Does everyone on the team know what they are responsible for?
- Is there anyone on the team that people avoid, or you do not have confidence in to do their job well?

Thinking about team health is important. How functional or dysfunctional is your team? Do people trust each other? Is there room for healthy conflict in an inclusive way... meaning everyone? Our tendency as leaders is to want people to all be adults and just get along. Be professional. Get things done. We get it. That said, it is our job as leaders to ensure that these things are happening as we expect and to intervene when needed. It is this intervention that many leaders are uncomfortable with, but if we do not address it, the problem will not fix itself.

Sometimes, within teams, a member is either underperforming or can become disconnected from the current priorities of the team. We tend to see examples of this in growing, start-up organizations where someone may have been an early leader and key to the organization. As the organization grows, they may not have the experience and skills necessary to lead at an enterprise level or lead large teams. How this is handled will both be an example of, and have an impact on, the organization's culture. Do you avoid the uncomfortable conversation but begin to marginalize their impact and access to driving key decisions and strategy? Do you find the right role for them whether that means moving to an advisory board or a different organizational role? Do you separate in a healthy way? Can you leverage their strengths and personal magic in a mutually impactful way? The goal is to set them and the rest of the team up for continued success. Avoiding the situation will not make it go away, and it's important both for their personal circumstances, and for the team and organization, that you find a resolution.

That might seem like an extreme example. In considering your team, look for examples or early indicators of tensions within the team so that you can bring the dialogue to the forefront, find solutions, and process those tensions before they disrupt your team and your culture.

Some common missteps that happen within teams include people reading into things that may not exist and/or making meanings based on their own experience and feelings. If this is happening to your team, assess if the reactions are consistent with the magnitude of the event or situation. This may be an early indicator that things seem fine on the surface, but there are things your team members aren't saying. Or that communication is an issue during and after decision making.

Organizational culture

Finally, let's examine your organizational culture. Without you or your team, there is no organization (we don't literally mean *you*, although it could be the case based on your circumstances).

The word *organization* actually means putting things together in a logical order. So, you need to organize your organization, starting with core values as the foundational building blocks. If you do not have them, create them. Then, build all HR programmes, processes, and policies using these core values as the foundation. This means that all components of your employee experience should be in alignment with these identified values. Often, people think that core values are for internal purposes only, but this could not be further from the truth. Consumers now expect that the customer brand and employer brand are in alignment, that a company's values set an expectation and commitment to both customers and employees alike.

> **A NOTE ON CORE VALUES**
>
> This is often a great opportunity to bring in a professional to help facilitate this process. If you don't have core values that really are alive in the organization and serve as the foundation for your culture, take the time to conduct a thoughtful process to develop them. Involve input from throughout the organization. It is not one or two people in a room making them up.
>
> One way to evaluate the effectiveness of your core values is to look at how decisions get made. When it comes to a tough decision, is there a clear alignment to the values? Does your organization know what values to rely

> on when making decisions? Are they empowered to prioritize customer service, or do they need to always only watch the bottom line? Do they know how to weigh differing priorities in those situations? Highly effective cultures define what is most important; the values guide people in feeling empowered to make decisions that will benefit the organization and they feel good doing so.
>
> Another consideration is to reflect on this potential scenario. If you have a leader who is consistently behaving in ways that are not in alignment with the stated values, is it addressed? Even if they are an important salesperson? If the bad behaviour is allowed to persist, your core values are being undermined. People will not have confidence in them or take them seriously. You might even be looking hypocritical without even knowing it.
>
> Done right, the result is values that people really identify with and see reflected in the day-to-day actions and behaviours of the culture. Ensure that you create an implementation plan that includes sustained communication and ways to integrate into various operational processes within your company. More on this in Chapter 4.

Once you have the core values and are creating the organization you want, then hold people accountable and be prepared to say goodbye to the ones who are not in consistent alignment with your core values. These people are ultimately undermining what you are working to build. The longer you keep them around, the more your purple unicorns, the ones who are high-performing rock stars, become disengaged, you will be perceived as less sincere, and the less credibility you will have.

The biggest challenges you face

You've no doubt read headlines touting, 'Be prepared for the future of work'. Or, 'The future of work will change jobs and talent'. If you are like us, the term 'future of work' makes you cringe. The pace of change means that it is not some distant possibility: it is *now*. What we outline here is what you need to do right now to keep up with the shifting business landscape for the way work is changing. You need to have thoughtful strategies in place today, especially when it comes to culture. Do you feel like you are fully prepared to handle the challenges? Is your team prepared? Is your organization prepared?

This is not a 'one-size-fits-all' solution, and it does not eliminate your secret sauce or what makes you and your organization unique. However, it does provide a path that, if followed, can result in increased business results. In fact, there is an opportunity to lean even further into the uniqueness of your culture and leverage that as a competitive advantage.

Companies today are being challenged to evolve. Even when they have very intentional cultures, we are seeing organizations that want to become more inclusive, have better-performing teams, and adjust to new employee expectations related to remote work and remote teams. When you think about these 'tweaks' that you may want to make, think about them broader than an initiative or current event, such as adding diversity and inclusion. Consider what key components need to be infused into your culture at a root level and how they will show up in your culture. For example, if diversity, inclusion and belonging are important enough to be a company value, how can you weave them into either the existing values or make demonstrative examples to the organization to show what is different and set the new expectations?

Adjusting is important to stay relevant and not get blindsided by major shifts in the external talent market or customer and employee preferences. Sustaining changes and having long-term communication plans to maintain the message are critical to success. Otherwise, organizations, just like individuals, will often revert to what has become habit or default behaviours.

How do we avoid this? It's important to not underestimate the significance of some of these potential tweaks. These can lead to major change management campaigns and for many organizations, that journey can be painful. We know that 70 per cent of change management efforts fail, so what can you do to have a higher chance of success? We recommend treating this as a major initiative if the change magnitude justifies it. In Chapter 10 we will outline some change management principles that will help you on your journey. Regardless of whether you are defining your culture for the first time or have recognized a need for the conscious evolution of your current culture, the components we'll walk through will help create a culture that weaves through the fabric of your organization, creating clarity, alignment, and all the benefits that a strong culture affords an organization. The result will be one of greater connection to your purpose within your organization.

This book will create a step-by-step system for you, your team, and your organization to facilitate change management, change agents, routines, and getting real. Your organizational culture will be transformed, aligned, and intentional.

Does this sound like a lot of work? Hell yes, it does. Will it be worth it? The answer depends on you. Do you want to build and sustain an organization where people want to work while achieving business results in an ever-changing work environment? If the answer is yes, then this journey will be worth it.

Just like the Yellow Brick Road to the Emerald City in *The Wizard of Oz*, there will be roadblocks and obstacles along the way. After all, what construction project is without its hiccups? But our systematic processes will overcome those roadblocks, provide questions to ask along the journey, and include assessments to gauge where you are today and how you get to where you want to be as an individual, team, and an organization.

We will provide tools to audit your current state, shape your desired thoughts, and operationalize an agile system that will support the sustainment of an aligned, high-performing culture.

However, this journey does not end once you close the book. You will need to check in with yourself, your team, and your organization to ensure there is still alignment (and if there isn't, determine how to course correct). Your culture will constantly be under construction if you want to build a sustainable organization. You will be adjusting and pivoting continuously and listening to internal and external inputs. Our aim is to help you feel confident and empowered with the tools to do so.

Common pitfalls

'I'm the Leader.' It is natural for leaders to think that just because they have said something that it should be. That people should just do it, without question. While we'd love to say this works, it often doesn't. Our role as leaders is to bring people along and be a 'leader' that others *want* to follow. This requires you to check yourself and your own behaviour; this is the pathway to getting others to do what you want them to do… start by looking within.

People should just do their work. Of course we want people to come to work and just get it done. We expect people to be professional and mature in the workplace. Some of that is reasonable, but organizations and teams are much more complicated than that. We need leaders who create a vision and who help people course correct when needed. The accountability piece is critical. Especially when you are an executive at the very top, if you don't hold someone accountable and ensure that things are happening the way they should or stand up when there is a leader behaving badly, who will? We've coached CEOs who don't want to be 'that guy (or gal)', but guess what…? You are. Even if you try to delegate to a Head of HR or a Chief of Staff, it won't work. People are looking to the leader themselves to set the standard of what is acceptable, what is expected and what isn't.

This is about work, not me personally. Why are we talking so much about you as a leader? Isn't this about work and about people being professional? Gone are the days (at least in most organizational cultures) where people would do things just because their leader asked or told them to. Positional power is no longer generally respected in itself, and especially is not impactful to inspire or motivate others to do things. Think about the best leader you have experienced in your career. What made them great? What was impactful about them? We can pretty much guarantee it was not their title. It is about the leader and their ability to be both authentic and vulnerable. It is about their ability to connect and inspire others. That is *all* about work and how work gets done.

Questions to ask

Gaining insight into the type of culture you want to create and your role in that culture is key before starting on the culture change journey. Below are some questions to ask yourself to develop a starting point.

QUESTIONS TO ASK – WHERE TO START WITH REGARDS TO YOUR CULTURE

- What is your organizational culture today? (This is for your eyes only. Be honest with yourself.)
- What is your desired organizational culture?
- How would you like people to communicate with one another?
- How would you like to see decisions made?
- What behaviours would you like people to demonstrate?
- Do all employees know the organizational values?
- Do people believe everyone lives the values in a consistent fashion?
- What happens if someone does not live up to a value (or behaves in a way that violates your core values)?
- How are decisions tied to your values both in decision making and in communication?
- What are the pillars of culture that are important to your organization?

QUESTIONS TO ASK – WHERE TO START WITH REGARDS TO YOUR ROLE IN CULTURE

- Have I set a clear vision about the culture I want to create within my team or organization?
- If I am clear about it, have I communicated it effectively to my key partners and stakeholders?
- How do I reinforce my commitment and vision of our culture?
- What bold examples do I have where my leadership behaviours or practices reinforce messages aligned with the desired culture?

- How can I get more information and feedback about my leadership impact and my impact on our team or organizational culture?
- Who are the other leaders that are key stakeholders in driving our organizational culture?
- How can I enrol them in this journey? (A SWOT analysis might help here to identify key supporters and even identify people who may resist your efforts; then create specific plans to engage them as appropriate. Avoiding resisters will not make them go away.)

Moving to action: what you can do next

Below are some actionable steps you can take today to begin thinking about understanding the complexity of your current organizational culture and how you may want to approach the journey ahead of you to create and sustain the culture you desire. Pick and choose which steps work for you. Some may be important now and others may need to wait. Come back to these next steps frequently to ensure you are making progress and moving in the right direction.

Involve others. Now that you have run through the questions above, a picture may be starting to take form. Leverage these questions to have some meaningful discussions with other key stakeholders as you work to understand what is really happening in your culture today.

Look for themes and low-hanging fruit. Between your own answers and the information you gain from others, look for key areas and themes. While we will take you on a journey covering a comprehensive look at the building blocks of culture, there may be some things that you can do now (or stop doing) that will have an immediate impact on your culture.

Start listening more. With your focus turned towards culture, you will start to hear things differently if you listen more. Listen in the hallway, the cafeteria, create opportunities to connect with people even if virtually. You may notice that you hear little indicators that relate to your company culture. These inputs are valuable clues that you might have missed previously. Ask more questions in meetings. Then be quiet and listen. Listen to what is said and what is not said.

Start to gather your thoughts, observations and insights from others that will help you as you continue on this journey.

Resist being a meaning maker. As you tune into these new channels, it will be tempting to make meaning of the various inputs you hear and observe. Use caution to not jump too quickly to root causes or simple resolutions. The key to a great culture is the way that all of these components work together. Solving a symptom might cause issues elsewhere. Work with a core team to thoughtfully design an approach to achieve the culture of your wildest dreams.

Lessons from the real world

What do your best leaders do to drive company culture?

> The word 'drive' doesn't seem to fit what our leaders strive to do. Maybe the better term is 'reveal'. Our leaders try to do their best daily, and even sometimes succeed, to emulate what we say we want leaders to behave like. That includes demonstrating a willingness to learn, to acknowledge those learning moments no matter the outcome and to be transparent in motivations. If our leaders reveal these characteristics, which means they are a fundamental part of that leader, then the chosen culture grows in kind.
>
> *Stan Sewitch, Vice President, Global Organization Development at WD-40 Company*

How do you integrate culture into your leadership operating model?

> We created a leadership competency model several years back, and 'builds culture' is one of the key tenets. We have integrated this model into our performance reviews and our leadership 360 process, so that culture remains top of mind for leaders, and so we're able to measure it year after year. Some of the specific items we look at are 'fosters open dialogue and collaboration,' 'provides the information people need to feel good about being a member of the team and organization,' and 'creates a feeling of belonging'.
>
> *Laurie Miller, Executive Vice President, Human Resources, Marketing and Communications at Alliance Healthcare Services*

Final thoughts

Our goal is that you feel empowered to set the direction of your own organizational culture. Identifying the role that you, your team, and the entire organization play in that is a first step. Getting real with yourself to assess your starting and desired points will magnify the results of your efforts.

Learning to identify indicators of both desirable and less than desirable cultures at a team and organizational level will increase your leadership impact. It will arm you with the foresight to take early action to course correct and coach others to do the same. Harnessing this collective power helps to operationalize this as a natural part of culture in itself.

It is not yours, or any one person's role to own culture. There has to be shared ownership and accountability to creating and maintaining the desired culture in alignment with the shared values. If you are looking to create momentum for a change, who will be your collaborators or your early adopters? Consider all groups of stakeholders. It would be great to identify them now and extend an invitation for them to join you on this journey.

02

Why top-performing cultures don't happen by accident

Smart companies and leaders don't leave culture to chance. Instead they invest in, nurture and foster culture in ways that make it easy for employees and customers to choose to engage with their brand. Purpose-driven cultures with clear 'values' work across all stakeholders and often enhance a company's value. Intangible assets are often a major part of an organization's market cap, and culture is clearly a part of that equation. Well-defined and driven cultures help produce sustained performance and superior returns over time.
CHARLIE PISCITELLO, CHIEF PEOPLE OFFICER AT ACUTUS MEDICAL, INC

For many companies, culture often takes a backseat to sales, marketing, product development, and market growth, and is made the priority solely for HR. In businesses where culture is paramount and made into a business priority (or even a goal or objective), it becomes everyone's priority. In short, organizational culture is aligned to the business strategy, and is an ongoing dialogue, especially at the executive level. If something isn't working, it is dealt with immediately, as opposed to waiting or issues being swept under the rug. This helps avoid the culture toxicity that results from issues remaining unaddressed for too long.

Good cultures cannot be faked or hurried. They are built intentionally. If we asked you, 'What do you want your culture to be?' how would you answer? Chances are you may say you want a positive culture, a good culture, or something along those lines. But, what does that mean? For example, if you want a positive culture, what behaviours do you want to see every day? Maybe it's one where employees treat each other with respect or one in which collaboration is encouraged and rewarded. Some words to describe a positive culture could include happy, upbeat, welcoming. While these are good adjectives to start, it is important for organizations and for leaders to dig deeper and really define the actions behind these words. Companies with strong cultures take a stand on culture and clearly define it. The leaders take an active role in defining it... and living it... and checking in to see if it still aligns with their values.

One of the biggest mistakes that leaders make is not getting specific enough. Defining culture should not be too broad. It is not about being all things to all people. It is about being *great* for the right people.

So, how do you get specific about culture? You ask questions. A few common questions that we often ask our clients are:

- What culture do we want to create?
- What specific behaviours will demonstrate this culture?
- What do we want employees to feel about our culture?
- How do we want employees and customers to be treated?
- What outcomes are important to us?

Notice how these are future-focused questions. We are talking about the ideal state, what an organization would like to see. From here, we shift gears and start talking about the present:

- How close are we to the culture we want to create?
- Do we have the right people in the right positions to help us achieve our desired culture?
- When we look at our leaders, do they consistently model behaviour aligned with the desired culture?
- What current policies, procedures and norms do we have that may need to be updated, changed, or eliminated?

Once these questions are answered, work to close the gap. This is where building a plan is important, and each of the areas we cover in subsequent chapters is written to help you design that plan.

Culture is a feedback loop

Good cultures have ongoing feedback from employees. For example, rather than waiting until months or even a year after someone has joined, Expedia gets immediate feedback from new employees and shares this with the executive team. Any adjustments are made quickly.[1] This is an example of making culture part of the ongoing dialogue and a key part of the operating system.

We are not talking about creating a feedback-friendly culture where employees are encouraged to ask for and give helpful feedback about performance, although that is definitely important to any culture. We are talking about actively asking employees their opinions about your culture; elements of the culture that are working well and elements that may need tweaking. This feedback allows organizations to adjust aspects of the culture that may be sending the wrong message or to continue programmes that are working.

Think back to a company you have worked for that had a strong culture. What were the first 30 days like there? What indicators did you have during your hiring and onboarding process that helped you integrate into the culture? Did you feel the same way after year one? How do you still feel today thinking back on that company? What you remember and how you feel is directly correlated to that organization's culture.

Top-performing cultures don't just write their values on the walls. They bring them to life in various policies and procedures, in how employees are rewarded and recognized, and in how the company operates and makes decisions. We will discuss this more in a future chapter.

Organizations with a good culture know that it needs to be retooled and refactored; it is not etched in stone. As circumstances change, the culture should be assessed. It is built on a strong foundation of values. Not only do organizations with strong cultures check in on the organization as a whole, these leaders check in with themselves as well. They understand that they are part of the ecosystem and their leadership needs to be developed and honed, just like the culture of the organization.

The role of leadership in culture

Think of culture and leadership as two legs of the organizational three-legged stool (the third being strategy). If any one of the legs is off, the stool will wobble and fall. While every employee has an impact on an organization, as we introduced in Chapter 1, leadership has the biggest impact on an organization's culture. Leaders need to embody the organization's values and engage employees to deliver on the organization's mission and vision. In fact, a leader's style can greatly affect the confidence of a team, impacting not only the team culture, but the organization's culture as a whole. Leaders set the tone for the work experience their employees will have.

If you asked three people what makes a good leader, chances are you wouldn't hear the same answer from all three, right? But, if you asked what makes a bad leader, you would have a bit more overlap on the answers. That is because it is easier to state what we don't like than identify what we do. Plus, it's easier to remember the bad leaders we have encountered in the past and recall how they made us feel.

> **CULTURE QUOTE**
>
> For a business leader to build a strong organizational culture, they must first look at themselves. As leaders, we must be willing to receive feedback, and to solicit feedback, so we can engage in self-reflection. We can't go through organizational change without being willing to change ourselves. Next, the leader should look to the other leaders in the organization, and ensure they are also open to change. It is absolutely critical that there is support from the top to build or change a culture, or the initiative will fail.
>
> *Tracie Sponenberg, Chief People Officer at The Granite Group*

According to a Hogan survey, bad managers comprise about 65 to 75 per cent of an organization's leadership level.[2] That means 7 out of every 10 leaders are considered poor managers! Hogan goes on to state that this poor showing of leadership may be due to a lack of judgement, the inability to gain trust and build teams, and an inability to relate to others and to learn and grow from mistakes. Now, if we are talking about organizational culture, what kind of tone are these leaders setting for the culture? What do their actions and behaviours convey to their employees and to others in the organization?

So, if it's easy to point out the traits of a bad leader, what does a good leader look like in relation to perpetuating a strong organizational culture?

First, in organizations with top-performing cultures, leaders connect on an emotional level with their employees to create motivation and a shared purpose. Employees want to know that their leader is aware of and appreciates the work they do for the team and the organization. They also want to feel valued, like what they do matters. Sadly, according to OC Tanner, an employee recognition company, only 59 per cent of employees feel that their leader values them.[3] They further go on to state that their research has shown that if the connection between employee and leader is weak, or even negative, employees often feel disconnected from other aspects of the culture. This just goes to show how important leadership is when creating a strong culture.

Second, leaders in top-performing cultures build trust. The strongest strategy and the best ideas can often fail if employees do not have trust in their leader. Why? Because without trust, employees are not motivated or engaged to produce results. The role of a leader is to show they are worthy of trust and that they trust in others. Leaders can build trust by allowing employees to make decisions, valuing their opinions, delivering consistent results, and giving consistent feedback. As will be discussed further later, perhaps the biggest way to earn trust as a leader is to ensure your actions and behaviours align with your core values and those of the organization.

Lastly, leaders in top-performing cultures understand their actions and the impact of those actions on the people around them. While leaders certainly aren't infallible, they know that what they say, how they say it and, most importantly, what they do, sets the tone and sends a message. Through the example they set, these leaders then help shape the culture in developing policies, structures and procedures based on those actions. These leaders also understand the consequences of their actions before they take the action. Their actions are intentional.

In summary, organizations with leaders who are self-aware have cultures that are high performing. Organizations with toxic cultures often have leaders who lack self-awareness, and so are ineffective and only concerned for their own well-being. The good news is leaders can build self-awareness and become assets for their organization in the culture-building process.

Building self-awareness

There are many definitions for self-awareness in leadership, and most are the same or similar in intent. The box below outlines traits of a self-aware leader. As you read through these, think about your own leadership style. What tone are you setting for your culture?

> TRAITS OF A SELF-AWARE LEADER
>
> - Recognize their own strengths and weaknesses to act in the best interest of their organization.
> - Lead with their strengths.
> - Surround themselves with people better than them, especially in areas that will leverage other people's strengths to offset their own weaknesses.
> - Operate in the best interest of the team and organization first.
> - Remain dedicated to goals and objectives by staying focused on the outcome and not being derailed by emotions.
> - Communicate and act in a positive manner upholding the highest standards of ethics and values.

- Have empathy.
- Ask a lot of questions for better understanding and development.
- Have a personal why.

As you read through these traits, did you notice a theme? They are focused externally more than internally. A self-aware leader knows they need to look at the larger picture and not just focus on their self-interest. The box below outlines what self-awareness is not.

WHAT SELF-AWARENESS IS NOT

- Knowing your strengths and using them to 'one-up' others.
- Perfection.
- Understanding your weaknesses and spending all of your time on 'fixing' those weaknesses.
- Something you 'complete.'
- Constant judgement of self.

In summary, self-awareness is about not being selfish. While self-aware leaders may not be perfect and may not have all of the answers (none of us do), they understand their actions have impacts on their team members and, more importantly, they want to make changes for the betterment of themselves, their teams, and their organization. Self-aware leaders understand their role and are active participants in shaping culture.

Psychology generally tells us that our core foundational beliefs in life are developed before we turn five years old. After the age of five, what we learn and what we experience is coloured by these core beliefs we hold in our subconscious. This means that reality is actually experienced differently by each of us.

What does this have to do with self-awareness? Well, these core beliefs rarely change throughout our lives, unless we put the necessary time, energy, and work into changing them. This work is the process of gaining self-awareness. The good news? This means you can absolutely increase self-awareness and become a better leader in the process.

From a leadership perspective, self-awareness makes leaders more cognizant of their emotions, behaviours, and biases. In turn, these leaders develop greater EQ (or emotional intelligence) in the process. In a report published by the *MIT Sloan Management Review* titled, 'How to Become a Better Leader', self-awareness was cited as the most important capability for leaders to develop.[4]

You may be asking how this relates to organizational culture. It may sound funny to say, but being a better leader and creating a better culture starts with turning the lens inward and focusing on ourselves first. It is not really that far-fetched an idea. Research has suggested that when we can see ourselves clearly, we are more creative. We make better decisions and our relationships are stronger. We are more confident and instil confidence in our employees. When was the last time you paused and took a moment to reflect on your own behaviours as a leader? Think about a recent encounter you had with someone in your organization. An encounter that perhaps did not go like you hoped. Now, imagine yourself on a balcony looking down at this interaction. How would you describe what you see? What does your body language convey? What messages are your words really sending? By going to the balcony, you are turning the lens inward and are better able to identify and adjust your actions in future interactions.

Awareness of our own weaknesses (or areas of opportunities) enables leaders to more effectively work with others who possess differing strengths and skills. These leaders are also more receptive to the ideas of others and the fact that those ideas may be better than their own. Conversely, a lack of self-awareness can potentially alienate others, caused by the impact one's actions can have. This alienation, especially when caused by a leader, can have a devastating effect on the organizational culture. We've all had those leaders who can see bad behaviour in others, but when you point out their behaviour, they are able to provide a list of reasons (also known as excuses) as to why they are different.

So, why does gaining self-awareness seem to be a challenge? It's simple, but definitely not easy. Sadly, sometimes the people who say they are the most self-aware are the ones who are furthest from it. Tasha Eurich, PhD, and her team conducted a self-awareness study with nearly 5,000 participants. Her research revealed that while most people believe they are self-aware, only 10 to 15 per cent are *actually* self-aware.[5] Let that sink in for a minute: 10 to 15 per cent. Why is that?

Establishing a baseline

It happens all the time. We think we are saying one thing, but what is being heard is completely different. As leaders, we need to be aware not only of the message we want to convey, but how we convey that message and the language we use. We all have filters. Remember, after the age of five, what we learn and what we experience is coloured by the core beliefs we hold in our subconscious. In turn, these experiences, in conjunction with our core beliefs, become our filters. These filters are how we experience the world and hear what is being said. None of us communicates in a vacuum.

One important distinction when gaining self-awareness is to consider our intent versus impact. We are not talking about being intentional (purposeful and thoughtful in behaviours and actions). We are talking specifically about communication. What you *think* you said versus what was *heard*. We have all given ourselves a pass when we misspeak or misstep, exclaiming, 'That's not what I meant!' What you hear depends on your filter. Imagine if the time taken to explain behaviour could be used for creating self-awareness and how that might redefine the term 'walk the talk'.

Intent versus impact is critical when talking about organizational culture. Leaders can have the best intentions, but if they lack the self-awareness to see the impact their actions and words can have on others, the end result could be doing more harm than good.

One way to gain a little self-awareness is to think about your own intent versus impact – think about your own behaviours and things you have said in the past. Review your behaviours from the past through your core values lens (the values you hold dear as a leader). As you reflect, ask yourself, 'Are my behaviours aligned with those values? Do my actions convey my intent?'

Then, think about your actions and behaviours today, in the present. Ask yourself the two following questions, again through the core values leader lens:

- What behaviours and actions am I not doing today that I should be doing to be more self-aware and aligned with my values?
- What behaviours and actions am I doing today that I should not be doing because they are not aligned with my values?

These can sometimes be hard questions to answer. If you are unsure of how to answer them, ask someone for their opinion. They will tell you. The goal is to get a better picture of what you think you are saying and doing and what you are actually saying and doing.

The journey of self-awareness helps leaders recognize their blind spots and then work to minimize them, thereby reducing miscommunication between our intentions and our actual impact. This journey is also part of the not-so-secret secret for creating top-performing cultures: it takes work. Leaders need to put in the work to reap the benefits.

No matter how long we have been in a leadership position, self-awareness is a learning journey without a final destination. Just like in the maps app on our mobile phones, we must enter a starting point before we can determine our path.

Ask yourself:

- What will I sound like as I gain self-awareness?
- How will my habits change?
- What words will I use?
- What will my actions look like?
- How would I want others to describe me?

Then consider:

- How will I get to my vision?
- What impacts will this process have on everything else going on day-to-day?
- How will my relationships be impacted (with my team, my clients, my peers)?

Finally, think about what success looks like. How will you know that you are gaining self-awareness?

There are many tools available that can assist us in building this self-awareness and creating a baseline. Various behaviour tests like Clifton Strengths, formerly Strengthfinders, E.Q 2.0, DiSC, Hogan, Myers-Briggs, etc have become popular because they are tools that assist with the process of self-reflection; they get us to turn the lens inward and focus on how we respond, react, and think. These tests also help determine how we make decisions and what motivates those decisions.

Self-awareness is not about being Zen or meditating or finding some ambiguous source of truth. It's about looking at your own behaviour and completing a self-audit of where you are at any given point in time and 'checking in' with yourself to see if that is where you want to be.

We often use the 'sleep test' as a check-in. Before bed, we will ask, 'Can I go to sleep knowing I made the best decisions I could with the information I had, and am happy about the way I treated people?' If the answer is no, we will ask, 'What could I have done better/differently? Do I need to have any additional conversations?' While we can't go back and change a decision or the way we acted, we can adjust our future behaviour.

Sometimes, in the moment, when a decision needs to be made, or we need to have a difficult conversation with someone, we'll ask, 'Can I sleep at night with the decision I'm about to make?' This is a critical question that we've asked ourselves, especially for big decisions that can impact the entire team. Our experience has shown us that leaders can quickly create a toxic culture by making big decisions in a vacuum or a silo.

The toxic culture lifecycle of a non-self-aware leader

When a decision is needed that affects the team, a bad manager does not consult the team. This lack of collaboration results in isolation of the leader and an inability to connect with the team, which creates an erosion in the team dynamic and the leader losing the team's trust. Once the trust is gone, the culture can quickly turn toxic, employees lose motivation, performance decreases, and business results suffer.

These behaviours then shape the entire culture and organization of the team. It's easy to see how this type of behaviour can quickly spiral out of control and cause employees, especially those high-performing employees, to quit and work elsewhere.

Not consulting your team (or utilizing a command and control leadership style) is just one example of the cause of a toxic culture, even when this happens without bad intent. Another unproductive leadership style is avoiding and tolerating. This tends to happen when a leader is more hands-off and provides an unstructured work environment. They also are unclear in their expectations and are more focused on pleasing others than doing what's right, or necessary. This can cause a toxic culture because employees can become insecure or fear the stability of their work environment. There is also an 'it's not my job' attitude closely followed by throwing colleagues under the bus and blaming others when something doesn't go right. When an organization has multiple leaders with this type of leadership style, unnecessary bureaucratic policies and procedures can be created, deflating the culture, and creating an environment full of individuals looking out for themselves versus an environment working together as one team.

These unproductive and toxic behaviours continue and are present in the majority of interactions the leader has with their team and with others throughout the organization. They assume everything is working well until something happens and one day, they realize they've been operating in crisis mode versus being proactive. They have continued making decisions like they have always made them and interacted with others like they have always done. Essentially, they have been operating with blinders on, completely unaware of the culture and interactions going on around them. This is how non-self-aware leaders perpetuate a toxic culture. It is not that their intentions are necessarily bad. It is just that they cannot see it. They are not tuned into themselves, or others, enough to see it.

Think about your leadership style. What is your leadership DNA? What is your organizational culture's DNA? How has your leadership style affected the culture?

CASE STUDY

Years ago, Hema worked for an organization where the CEO, let's call him Ben, would berate his executive assistant for not being available EVERY TIME he called and needed something. He would publicly criticize his field sales reps for not achieving 120 per cent of their revenue quota. Ben didn't see anything wrong with his behaviour and was happy that these 'low performing' employees were leaving the organization. According to Ben, their lack of motivation and reasons for being unhappy were intrinsic and not caused by him. After 65 per cent of the sales force turned over, the organization was viewed as toxic, it was difficult to recruit new employees, and profitability suffered. A few years after Hema left, the organization shut their doors.

Think of organizational culture like a bank account. There are credits and debits. Strong values, high-performing teams, and self-aware, highly accountable leadership teams are credits. They increase your bank balance and make employees happy, resulting in increased productivity. On the flip side, values misalignment at an executive and HR level, poor leadership, and constantly shifting priorities are all debits. They decrease the strength of the organizational culture and create unhappy and disengaged employees. In turn, these debits take away from business results.

Don't believe us? Economists conducted various studies with over 700 employees. What they found is that happy employees are 12 per cent more productive than unhappy, disengaged employees. In fact, unhappy employees cost US businesses over $300 billion each year![6] If our non-self-aware leader from the previous example was self-aware, how different would those results be?

As discussed earlier in this section, the good news is that behaviours can be changed, and non-self-aware leaders can gain self-awareness with time and practice.

The high-performing culture lifecycle of a self-aware leader

A self-aware leader consults the team when a decision needs to be made that affects everyone. This type of leader understands they cannot make decisions in a vacuum and if they want to keep their team's trust, they must make the team part of the decision-making process. In so doing, the team feels valued and heard, continuing to build trust with the leader. In turn, this trust creates a high-performing team that is motivated to deliver.

CASE STUDY

We once worked with a client who had to make some difficult decisions on his team. The organization was undergoing layoffs and he needed to cut his team by 45 per cent. He spoke to his leaders and was honest about what was occurring within the organization and why it was happening. While it was not easy to hear, the other leaders understood the difficult position their manager was in. Two of the leaders stated that while they loved their jobs and the leader, they would rather have their positions eliminated, as their teams were fully capable of continuing without them and would rather save the jobs of their team members. Due to complete self-awareness and open communication, they were able to navigate this difficult time and work through it – not around it.

The above example is not just about the self-awareness of the CEO. It is about the self-awareness of the other leaders as well. A high-performing culture is created because employees see these behaviours, and although every situation isn't a positive one in the case of layoffs, the employees see how the leaders put their own feelings and well-being aside for the betterment of the whole.

People are watching

As a leader, people are watching you (probably more than you think). You may think that people don't see the impacts and nuances of your actions or don't have visibility, but think again. This visibility applies to how you treat yourself, treat others, and how you allow others to treat you. Just as your kids will follow your actions much more than your words, the same is true with your workforce. People are making meaning of what you do and say, as well as what you do not do or say.

Nothing derails a company culture more quickly than leadership behaviour that is misaligned with company values. If you're being disrespectful to your employees but telling your employees that respect is important, what message are you really sending?

What you are really saying is, 'The rules don't apply to me. Do as I say, not as I do.' And there it is. The misalignment.

One place a values misalignment can be really evident is within an HR team. Your HR team is helping shape and lead the culture. They are infusing your organization's core values throughout all policies, procedures, programmes, and systems. And if they're not, they should be. So, if you have a misalignment with company values within your HR team, you can expect to read about it on Glassdoor, exit surveys, engagement surveys, and anywhere else employees are providing feedback.

If the 'powers that be' aren't self-aware, then how can they be expected to develop their own organization, create a high-performing culture, or bring out the best performances in their talent?

Behaviour needs to be managed as actively as company financials are. If leadership behaviour is misaligned with the company culture and values, and that behaviour is not addressed in a timely manner, there are impacts on the entire organization, which can derail performance, profitability, and strategy.

As we mentioned before, while we can't control the behaviour of others, we, as leaders, can control our own behaviour by turning the lens inward. We can also have open and frank discussions with our leaders and employees about their behaviour. In so doing, we are addressing the bad behaviour as it arises and making it part of the organizational daily dialogue. In other words, we are operationalizing self-development and culture while processing organizational tensions as they come up.

This is especially important at the leadership level. Oftentimes, you as the leader may have the last word and others may not challenge you. But how is this helping the organization? Developing self-awareness helps us build teams and understand the motivations of others. We can then put our team members in positions that play to their strengths. A self-aware leader will embrace the challenge and require it in a respectful and healthy way, so the decisions being made are the best ones for the team and the organization.

The more you know yourself, the better choices you will make. The better choices you make, the better the organizational culture and the better the culture, the better the performance of your team. It really is *that* simple. Take a look at the questions in the box below. Think about your own leadership style as you answer the questions.

HOW SELF-AWARE ARE YOU?

- What visible actions do you consistently take to demonstrate company values?
- How often do you give feedback?
- How often do you ask for feedback?
- How do you react when you make a mistake?
- How do you react when someone on your team makes a mistake?

Common pitfalls

From our experience, it's easy for organizations to become complacent with their culture. The saying, 'If it's not broken, why fix it?' may come to mind. The truth is, culture can make or break the success of your organization and should be actively looked at and improved upon. Below are a few common pitfalls to look out for when designing your ideal culture.

Culture can be 100 per cent crafted. The short explanation here is that it can't. Leaders most definitely set the vision and direction of the culture. They help define what it should look like. The problem is that leaders often think they can script, and therefore control, every piece of the organization's culture. This does not happen for two reasons. First, behaviours. CEOs cannot control the actions or words of every leader and employee within their organization. Culture provides the framework for how people should act and behave. Ultimately, the final decision is on them. Second, pieces of your organizational culture will need to remain organic as they will ebb and flow as your organization grows and matures.

Focusing on the negatives. If there are aspects of your culture that you would like to change, don't walk around complaining about them. Instead focus on the positive – the outcome you would like to see.

Not providing the tools. Once you have outlined the ideal culture you would like to create, be sure to build tools and resources into your plan for rollout. One area that CEOs and other leaders often underestimate is the need to properly train managers, and all employees, in the behaviours that are critical to your new high-performing culture. Culture change is all about behaviours. Use the next eight chapters to not only help you build a plan for creating a high-performing culture, but to also provide areas in which to train employees and managers.

Moving too quickly. Think about the time it's taken for you to create the culture you have today. It did not happen overnight. Whether you are a mature organization, or a start-up and your organization is still in its infancy, think about slowing down to speed up. Be deliberate and intentional in how you define and create your culture. Moving too quickly and wanting to 'get it done' can actually do more harm than good. Other than the obvious – employees thinking it's an item on a checklist – you can miss critical areas that may unintentionally send the wrong message (ie not thinking through all of the necessary HR policies that will need to be updated in conjunction with a culture change).

Taking yourself too seriously. Top-performing cultures have fun and laugh. They encourage friendships and answer to the social needs of employees. In our work we've seen two extremes. On one side, there are organizations who are all about fun with their ping pong tables and beer taps. On the other side, there are organizations who think high-performing cultures are created because they focus on business all the time and because employees work a lot of hours (and at all hours of the day and night). These are not hallmarks of a top-performing culture. In fact, these are hallmarks of a dysfunctional and potentially toxic culture. Finding the balance is key. It is important to remember to have fun and create a positive culture where people feel welcome and authentic.

Questions to ask

Creating a sticky culture means your employees are happy, engaged, and high performing, and so are more inclined to recommend their friends and others in their network to work for your organization. Top-performing companies have figured out what keeps employees engaged and successful, and so have made their culture sticky.

These top-performing cultures treat culture like an active event. As we've said before, culture is not a 'set it and forget it' strategy. You constantly have to come back to it, check in with it, tweak it and reassess again.

Below are some questions to ask, of yourself and of your employees, to better gauge the culture's stickiness and your leadership behaviours.

QUESTIONS TO ASK YOUR EMPLOYEES

- What is one aspect of our culture that you really enjoy?
- In your opinion, what is our 'secret sauce' – that one aspect of our culture that makes us special?

- Do you think our culture is high performing? Why or why not?
- If you could change one aspect of our culture, what would it be and why?
- Other than a paycheck, what keeps you coming back here every day? What motivates you to work for us?

QUESTIONS TO ASK YOURSELF

- For my organization (your specific department or the organization as a whole) am I seeing high, average, or low turnover rates for our industry?
- How many of our new employees are coming through referrals?
- Am I promoting growth?
- Am I promoting a culture that encourages a life outside of work?
- How am I tapping into and leveraging the strengths of those on my team?

Moving to action: what you can do next

So, if you think top-performing cultures just happen, then we're sorry to say that you would be incorrect. They take time. They take perseverance. They take failures. There is no universal culture, and companies with top-performing cultures do not have a secret formula that they are hiding from the rest of the world. However, these organizations do give culture a starring role (not just a supporting role). Culture happens by design, not by accident.

To support you on your journey to creating a top-performing culture, we have created some actionable steps you can take today to use what we have discussed here. As each journey is unique, pick and choose which steps work for you: some may be important now and others may need to wait. We recommend coming back to these next steps frequently to ensure you are making progress and moving in the right direction.

Make culture part of the daily dialogue. As a leader, don't avoid the elephant in the room. If there is organizational tension that needs to be addressed, or bad behaviour for that matter, talk about it. Resolve it. Don't sweep it under the rug or leave it unaddressed. Both will only make it worse. And employees will see there is an issue.

Develop a practice for gaining self-awareness. Can I give you some feedback? Did you cringe a little when you read that? The word *feedback* has some serious negative connotations. When we hear this, we expect that what will follow will be a judgement, unsolicited advice, an opinion, or, worse yet, 'constructive' criticism. This doesn't always have to be the case. Feedback can help inform our future decisions, *and* feedback is not always about you. It's more someone else's interpretation of something you said or did. What if you didn't wait until someone asked if they could give you feedback? When was the last time *you* asked for feedback? How useful the feedback was that you received depends on how effectively you asked for it. When asking for feedback, communicate that you would like honest, truthful feedback. Communicate why you are asking – so you can improve in the future. Then stop talking and listen. Listen deeply, do not interrupt, and ask clarifying questions so you properly understand the feedback that is being provided. Receiving feedback is not about judging what someone else is saying. Most importantly, write down what was said so you can think about it and apply it in the future. Then, say thank you!

One suggestion that might make these meetings a little more comfortable is to have a set of questions prepared that you ask each person you meet with. This will help you get a more holistic perspective of how you are viewed today. A few questions to include in your informational one-on-ones are: How would you describe the culture of our (team/organization)? What do I do well that fosters an environment of teamwork, accountability, leadership? What could I improve if I want to see a culture that has more of those things? Do I hold leaders accountable for their behaviours? Can you share an example of where I did that well? Where I did not? What advice do you have for me? Is there anything I didn't ask you that you think I should know?

Go to the balcony. Sometimes we need to gain perspective and to look at our behaviours and actions as if we were watching a play unfold. What is your role in the play? How do the actions of others negatively or positively affect you? How does this manifest itself in your subsequent actions and behaviours? Take a close look at patterns because these tell a story. Going to the balcony can be hard. It is not a 'one and done' exercise; you will alternate between participating in the action and going to the balcony throughout the day. This exercise will help you gain perspective, which allows us to pause and ensure that the decisions we *think* we're making, the actions we *think* we're taking, or the statements we *think* we're saying are all actually being received in the manner we intended. This view also allows us to be less reactionary and to take a more thoughtful approach to our leadership. And, in turn, create a high-performing culture.

Consider getting a coach. The truth is, we can all benefit from a coach. Throughout our careers, we have both had coaches. We may stay with one for a few years, take a break, and then decide we need to find a new coach based on where we are in our lives. Gaining clarity and self-awareness can be a daunting task on your own and that's when a coach can really help. A coach is not a therapist. We repeat: a coach is not a therapist. By providing clarity, a coach can help you achieve short- and long-term organizational goals while guiding you to find and define your leadership style. A coach will not do the work for you. Finding the right coach is what's important. Interview a few. Ask other business leaders whom you admire and respect if they have any recommendations. And, when you find a coach, do not be afraid to speak up and tell them what you want to talk about and where you need clarity. Coaches will help you conduct 360s or other assessments that help you understand how you are perceived and how to interpret the feedback, identify themes and potential derailers. They will also help you prioritize an action plan on what to work on first in your journey of self-awareness and leadership effectiveness.

Lessons from the real world

What is one thing leaders can do immediately to create a high-performing culture?

> Organizational leaders (in alignment with each other) can clearly define and articulate the culture they want to promote to employees, sharing the rationale behind it, eg what's working and what's not that impedes organizational success and productivity. Included in communicating what the preferred culture looks like, leaders need to share their strategy, vision, values, performance expectations, and expected behaviours. Research shows that successful culture change entails a proactive approach to managing the human elements of change. It proves that employees are more likely to embrace and adopt change when the following conditions are in play: they know what is expected of them; they have the awareness, emotional intelligence, skills, and tools to succeed at meeting expectations; they are incentivized/rewarded to make the discretionary effort; and they are held accountable for meeting expectations.
>
> *Kathy Naylor, Global Human Capital and Business Transformation Adviser and Executive Coach at Change and Leadership Solutions*
>
> Define success (otherwise known as measurement). I am shocked time and time again when I show up to help low-performing teams and companies, to see how little they define what is expected. People need to know what great looks like. Leaders often have an idea in their mind, and never communicate it to anyone. Employees often have a clear idea of what they think is expected, but never double check with their leaders. In the end both parties are disappointed, and the company gets a poor outcome. Define success!
>
> *Chris Dyer, Performance Consultant, Bestselling Author and CEO at PeopleG2*

What is one way leaders can gain self-awareness?

> Bonding! In every meeting of 30 minutes or more, ask each person to answer, 'How are you showing up?' Make sure senior people go last. At the end of the meeting ask, 'How are you leaving?' In the first question

we can find out where our people are as they enter. If you find someone in need of help, in distress, exhausted, etc, you might need to excuse them, cancel the meeting, or stop and deal with their emotional needs. When you leave and ask the second question (again senior people go last), you will find out if your perceptions about the meeting align with theirs. We often think everyone 'got it', and when I ask this question, I find out some of them did not. That's ok, at least I know they need more help, time, or training. This one addition to any meeting will up your EQ as leader and increase self-awareness by 500 per cent.

Chris Dyer, Performance Consultant, Bestselling Author and CEO at PeopleG2

Final thoughts

It is important to remember that, while you can't control how other people react and what they say or do, you do have 100 per cent control over your own actions, behaviours, and reactions. This is especially important if you have members on your team who are not self-aware and who are still finding their way. Stay present when you are in stressful situations and remain aware of your own emotions. This is how you will contribute to creating a top-performing culture.

Before moving on, take a few minutes to write down two to three key takeaways from this chapter with regards to your organizational culture. Think about aspects of your culture that you may need to consider changing. Now, looking at that list, next to each takeaway write down one action item that you will commit to doing to move your culture in the right direction.

What will you do?

Endnotes

1 Ballezza, J (2015) Asking for employee feedback should start on day one, *Glassdoor*, 21 January, https://www.glassdoor.com/employers/blog/asking-employee-feedback-start-day-one/ (archived at https://perma.cc/FX7D-MZ7K)

2 Hogan Assessments (2009) HPI + HDS combining assessment to predict job performance, https://237jzd2nbeeb3ocdpdcjau97-wpengine.netdna-ssl.com/wp-content/uploads/2016/12/HPI_HDS_ROI.pdf (archived at https://perma.cc/TB2Y-L7KA)

3 OC Tanner (2019) How does leadership influence organizational culture? 23 October, https://www.octanner.com/insights/articles/2019/10/23/how_does_leadership_.html#:~:text=Leaders%20have%20a%20tremendous%20impact,achieve%20personal%20and%20professional%20success (archived at https://perma.cc/E46P-SFCV)

4 Toegel, G and Barsoux, J (2012) How to become a better leader, *MIT Sloan Management Review*, 20 March, https://sloanreview.mit.edu/article/how-to-become-a-better-leader/ (archived at https://perma.cc/8P4E-FUHS)

5 Eurich, T (2018) What self-awareness really is (and how to cultivate it), *Harvard Business Review*, 04 January, https://hbr.org/2018/01/what-self-awareness-really-is-and-how-to-cultivate-it (archived at https://perma.cc/LXD4-JBFG)

6 Oswald, A, Proto, E and Sgroi, D (2015) Happiness and productivity, *Journal of Labor Economics*, http://wrap.warwick.ac.uk/63228/7/WRAP_Oswald_681096.pdf (archived at https://perma.cc/CRE2-3RK7)

03

Organizational structure

Effective organizational culture is based on the delicate balance of mission and the organization's unique mix of relationships and values. Creating and maintaining effective organizational culture is a continual dance – more of an art than a science. When in balance the tempo, harmony, and melody make beautiful music and translate organizational 'goodness' into 'greatness'.

DR SUNITA 'SUNNY' COOKE, SUPERINTENDENT/PRESIDENT AT MIRA COSTA COMMUNITY COLLEGE DISTRICT

Okay, so now that you have a foundational understanding of organizational *culture*, it is time to think about your organizational *structure*. The reason we go here so quickly is that organizational structure should be a driver of culture. Getting it right will align the organization to successfully drive business strategies. At its core, organizational structure is a workplace hierarchy. It defines how jobs and tasks are completed in order to reach the organization's objectives. The right structure also helps attract and retain the right talent to help you achieve those business priorities. Therefore, the structure needs to support and enable the desired culture.

You as a leader play a fundamental role in building a healthy, functioning, high-performing organization driven by the organizational structure. Think of your team structure today. Does it support the culture you want to create? Does it enable the culture you want or the one you want to move away from? If you are not sure how to answer these questions, here are some things to consider:

- Are decisions made in a clear way by people who have the information to make the best decisions?
- Does your organization have a high level of accountability?
- Are your leaders clear about their roles and responsibilities?
- Are your employees clear about their roles and responsibilities?
- Where are your customers? Who maintains those relationships?

Intellectually, we know that the people within our organization are key to whether a company succeeds or fails. We also know that great leadership is what will ensure that we meet our strategic commitments and what will inspire our teams to bring their best discretionary effort by choice.

If organizations want to succeed and create exceptional cultures, they need to stack the deck (aka build their team) in a new way. To do this, organizations have to start thinking about talent differently.

Types of organizational structures

There are many organizational structures, but knowing all of them is not important, unless you are in HR (in which case you should have a good understanding of most structures). Figure 3.1 outlines a short

FIGURE 3.1   Most commonly used structures

Functional Units are formed according to major technical or professional function performed	**Product-based/ lines of business** Units are formed around each of the major products (or services)	**Customer or geographical area-based** Units are formed around the characteristics or location of customers or markets
Business process teams/agile Cross-functional teams structured around the major work processes	**Matrix** Units are formed where individuals have accountability to two managers: one functional and one project/product/geo	**Hybrid** Units are formed which mix and match the above structures to create the best fit to their environment

list of some of the most commonly used structures. Consider where your own organization sits from a structural perspective.

Functional. This structure is one of the most common structures we see. Employees are segregated into their functional departments, each with a leader, eventually reporting up to the CEO. This type of structure builds functional excellence and a depth of experience. There is consistency in processes and clear career paths.

Product-based/lines of business. This type of structure emphasizes the product and, due to this focus, creates more innovation. For organizations with multiple products, this type of structure is scalable.

Customer or geographical area-based. This structure creates a localized focus and allows for the organization to adapt products and services to local differences. Accountability can be fairly straightforward as a regional leader coordinates and oversees all of the activity in a given region.

Business process teams/agile. This involves a flatter structure where employees are empowered to make decisions and innovate. It has a customer-centric focus and is easily scalable and highly adaptable based on market shifts.

Matrix. This structure often works for start-ups where resources are scarce and employees wear multiple hats. There is a lot more collaboration and flexibility in this structure and it also allows for diverse perspectives to come to the table to solve problems.

Hybrid. Think of this type of structure as a customized structure based on your organizational needs, priorities and industry. You can combine the best pieces of the above structures to create one that best fits your needs.

While you do not need to become the expert in each of these, what you *do* need to know is how your organization works. As you considered the various common organizational structures above, were you able to identify which one represents your company? Who does what? Who should report to whom and why? Do you have departments? Are your departments set up functionally? Is that effective for the way you work? Do you have regions, products, or geographies?

Where and how do decisions get made? Do leaders have manageable team sizes? What are the channels and cadences of communication?

All of these items are important in determining an organizational structure that is right for your organization. The answers to each of these questions depend on the type of culture you want to create.

What's structure got to do with culture?

Structure has everything to do with culture. The organizational structure informs the organizational processes. These processes inform the metrics, both at an organizational and individual level. All of these combined attract the right type of people for your organization to help you achieve your business strategy and priorities.

If you want a culture built on process and hierarchy, you may opt to have a more traditional, organizational structure with multiple spans and layers (individual contributor reports to a manager, who reports to a senior manager, who reports to a director, who reports to a senior director, who reports to a… well, you get the picture). In this common, functional structure, there is a marketing department for all marketing employees, an HR department for all HR employees, an IT department, and so on. Consider how the structure fosters (or not) communication across functional lines. Does your organization operate in a siloed fashion? If so, how does the culture drive or support that? Do people think of themselves as many separate, individual teams or as one big one? Perhaps you want a culture that holds all employees accountable for their own decision making and gives them the power to make decisions. In this case, *fewer* spans and layers would be beneficial, and perhaps a matrix organization may make the most sense. What type of culture is actually being supported by the current structure? Long story short… structure matters.

The type of structure an organization has can also depend on where in their lifecycle they may be. Start-ups may not have a clearly defined organizational structure, allowing them to move quickly and maintain agility, or they may have a functional structure. As they expand, grow, and add new products and services, they may decide that a product-based (or line of business-based) structure is best, where units are formed around each of the major products or services. These adjustments can be hard as people shift from wearing many hats to having to select one or two to specialize in and be accountable for. For many international companies, a geographical structure may be best, centred around the characteristics or location of markets.

There is no one-size-fits-all organizational structure, and there is no right or wrong answer. Structures really are dependent upon each organization and can vary even within one organization.

SIX THINGS TO CONSIDER WHEN LOOKING AT ORGANIZATIONAL STRUCTURE

- *Management attention*: Force attention to a critical outcome by elevating it in the structure. What areas need more attention?

- *Specialization*: Differentiate or separate out a role/group by expertise or functional activity. Are there areas that require focused leadership (ie regulatory)? Look for potential redundancies in the organization (ie do you have a centralized finance department with business analysts embedded within departments?).

- *Coordination and integration*: Assure an integrated, whole outcome. Is there enough support for employees to enable the integration and necessary outcomes?

- *Leveraged resources and cost*: Create more impact and/or economies of scale by consolidating resources. Where are there redundancies (ie FP&A)?

- *Control and accountability*: Place a clear and visible point of authority and control over key results. What are the rules for accountability?

- *Motivation and development*: Create roles that are motivating and provide high degrees of development experience. Are there proper incentives in place? Do the incentives align to drive the desired results, or do they unintentionally drive conflicting behaviour?

Once you have an organizational structure that will enable business success, it is important to think about the roles within that structure.

If you build it, they will come

Defining the roles within an organizational structure is extremely important. What's more is that defining these roles should be a conscious effort, one that is prioritized and taken seriously. Clearly defining the roles has an immediate positive impact on culture – it ensures that all employees know what they are doing and what is expected of them. This clarity means people know how to behave. It sounds simple because it is simple, yet many organizations unfortunately leave it up to chance. The right, clearly defined role will attract the right type of person. Getting it wrong at this stage could derail the culture and take time to course correct.

How can finding the right talent, regardless of source, have any derailers or potential downsides? Oftentimes, our first instinct is to blame the employee, the talent we hired. If we hire a full-time employee, we often think we may have been better off upgrading the position or finding a consultant. If we partner with a consultant, we often think we may have been better off hiring a full-time employee. The truth is, it's not the type of talent, or how you stack your deck, that has the downside – it's what leads you to finally think about talent differently. What we are saying is that it starts with you.

When someone leaves or you have a new open position, is your first thought, 'I must fill it immediately'? What about your direct reports? Do they think every position on their team must be filled because they have always had those positions? While the organizational structure is only as strong as the talent that fills the roles, all roles do not always need to be filled and certainly not in the same exact way as they have always been. This is where it's important to break out of our old cycles and ways of thinking. As a leader, if you allow this type of thinking to occur then you will continue getting the same results, and nothing will change.

Instead of quickly trying to fill a role when someone leaves, pause instead. Do not immediately react. First, think about your current business strategy and key priorities. What upcoming key deliverables are required in the near term? Then think about the position, the requirements for the role (more on that later), and the future of the department and organization. Is the role, in its entirety and as it is today, needed to achieve the departmental and overall organizational goals? If the answer to that question is no, then take some time to review the position and what is needed. If you had to redesign this role, what would it look like? Ensure your direct reports and other leaders do this as well. Identify what skills and capabilities your organization needs when you look three to five years to the future – is this an opportunity to invest in skills that you need but don't have or to make an opportunistic hire in a key area of focus? Also, we know that employees want career growth and that it is not always vertical growth. Is there an opportunity for lateral or rotational movement within the company?

As you start to define roles, think about what your job descriptions are saying. Job descriptions outline the necessary skills, roles, responsibilities, certifications, and degrees. Once these job descriptions are in the hands of the recruiters, they are sourcing and calling candidate after candidate, checking to see if they meet the qualifications and have the necessary experience in all areas listed. But how often do we stop to consider whether all of those skills listed are mandatory, whether the college degree trumps the necessary experience, whether the whole role is necessary as a full-time position versus being broken down into its parts?

These job descriptions are the first visibility and insight candidates have into your organization and culture. What do your job descriptions say about you? Job descriptions should be structured as a marketing tool to recruit the kind of people you want to attract to your culture. That means explaining what it feels like to work for your organization. What kind of behaviours are you looking for? What can someone who might apply expect in working there? What do their first 30, 60, 90 days on the job look like? How you write your job descriptions drives the type of people that apply. Job descriptions are a good tool to communicate that you value diverse opinions, experiences and viewpoints. We will talk more about diversity, inclusion and belonging in Chapter 9, but it's important to say here that finding ways to design your roles that will increase the funnel of qualified talent will give you an advantage in this area and maybe open up more channels for greater diversity of all kinds: experience, perspective, thought, gender, race and more.

Alongside this, you should consider what your company perspective is on college degrees. Does your company have a standard clause for every role, 'College Degree Required' or 'Graduate Degree Preferred'? Is that really true for every role? The value we each place on a college education is personal and multi-faceted. Many people acknowledge that the social skills and the commitment we demonstrate and learn by completing a college education are valuable, but how critical is the value of what we actually learn sitting in a classroom and its importance for our ability to complete a job to the best of our abilities? In actuality, the answer is that it varies, and the perceived value of college degrees is changing within the talent landscape. In the United States, most job descriptions list 'four-year degree' as a minimum requirement. But, when looking at each position in your organization, how important is a college degree versus experience, certifications, and the ability and willingness to learn?

There is not necessarily a right or wrong answer to this. It is a philosophical question and one that may differ based on the role and company. For example, we certainly want our doctors to have gone to and graduated from medical school. But what about a computer programmer? Is a college degree necessary if they possess certifications and the right coding skills? Can life experience count in ways that a college degree can't? The point is to be open to how you structure your organization and not unintentionally close yourself off to segments of the workforce who may have other skills, capabilities, and values. Again, just because you have *always* hired people with a college degree, doesn't mean it's the right decision moving forward. Be aware of how the higher education market is changing and the impact that is having on people's choice of going to college. The shifts happening in this area are significant and it's critical that you are aware of and acknowledge the changing landscape so that you can adjust your job descriptions and required qualifications based on what will best support your company's success.

Think about the open roles you have in your organization right now. Beyond the college degree, are all those 'must haves' listed on the job description truly must haves? How do these represent and affect the culture of the team? How about the culture of the organization? Yes, there are definitely some 'must haves' for most if not all roles: items like clear, open and honest communication or the ability to multi-task. But what do these even mean and how do they apply to your organization? One item to consider is whether these types of 'must haves' are just lip service, and you now have people in your organization today who do not have clear, open and honest communication or who can't effectively multi-task. Instead of a laundry list of skills someone needs to have, consider reframing these items in the context of your core values, which we will discuss in the next chapter. For example, consider adding phrases such as, 'We value honesty in all communications, both verbal and written.' Phrases such as this communicate your culture, your values and what is expected of someone in the role. This is not a 'must have' skill but an expectation of anyone that works for your organization.

Is your goal to find the best talent for your organization? The talent pool is automatically narrowed when we add limiting characteristics, such as a college degree, a particular college degree, or 10 to 15 skills that someone needs to be stellar at. You may unnecessarily limit your pool of rock stars and pass over candidates who are highly skilled at getting the job you want done. If the point is to build the best team you can, keep an open mind about where that talent is coming from.

Redefine your project

As you dissect roles and job descriptions, assess projects and how work is organized. There are definitely some positions or jobs where the entire role is necessary as all pieces fit together. But is the same true of projects? Do you need to hire a full-time employee to complete the entire project, including those aspects they may not be fully qualified for? Projects can be broken down into specific tasks; the most effective example of this is in construction. When redoing your house, you have a painter, a carpenter, an electrician, and maybe someone who does tile work. Rarely are these the same person. That is because each is skilled at their unique craft. They have spent years honing their skills and developing processes and systems that allow them to be the best at what they focus on. Think of your projects the same way and consider the skills and roles you need in your team accordingly.

Using the same illustration, who manages this team of experts? Usually there is a General Contractor, someone who knows enough about each of these components to know what good looks like, manage a schedule, motivate the team, hold people accountable, set a vision for the end deliverables and results and finally execute. Who would fill this position for projects you're involved in?

Before you fill an open position and hire employees, break the project down into separate actionable tasks. This is referred to as task management. Task management allows you to take the often vague, unclear and extremely large project goals and break them down into clear and descriptive tasks. When you've done this, assess which option would be most effective. You could hire one or two employees who are great at various pieces of the project and make them responsible for the entire thing. Or you could consider hiring a freelance worker for each separate task who is specially trained to perform that task. If you have a strong project manager, they can manage the skilled workers and deliver quality results, potentially at a fraction of the cost or with greater specialized experience than you might have internally. Plus, when creating teams consisting of diverse talent made of full-time employees and gig workers, you are creating meaningful work for everyone, boosting motivation and engagement by tapping into the strengths of each individual. Perhaps by allowing people to have diversity in their assignments or engage on projects or growth tasks, we can increase engagement and reduce the risk of people feeling like they need to leave the organization for career growth and opportunities. You can create your own internal gig economy, which can do wonders for culture!

Pausing to think about what you really need, the time frame that the work needs to be done in, and what kind of talent is best to do it will allow you to make better decisions about the kinds of resources you bring into your organization and how you engage them in your culture. It also leads to more proactive and consciously constructed structure and culture. You are removing yourself and your direct reports from auto-pilot and taking a much more active role in defining who you want to be and how you need to work.

> **CULTURE QUOTE**
>
> It's going to be harder to speak openly, directly, and honestly just at a time when it's needed most. People are more divided (politically, economically, educationally, ideologically, etc). People/leaders are uncertain about the future. We have less physical contact and are working remotely, especially due to COVID-19. This can cause people to say less, play things closer to the vest, speak more generally and dance around issues. When you have trust and strong relationships, you can speak more openly. My advice for a strong culture... build trust. Speak more openly.
>
> *Joel Stern, Senior Talent Acquisition Business Partner, Cue Health*

A new kind of team

One important facet of organizational structure is the structure and effectiveness of the team. Team dynamics greatly affect not only the team culture and the larger organizational culture, but also the engagement and performance of employees.

Some might ask, what constitutes a team? While it may make you think about your actual (full-time permanent) employees, today we have even more options in who composes our teams and how we source our talent. You have likely heard of it, the trend in the workforce that goes by many names: the gig economy, independent workers, free agent workers, elastic talent, agile talent, or on-demand talent. We touched on it above when we talked about projects and task management.

The days of joining a company and staying with them for life are mostly gone. People who moved for career advancement or changed jobs to gain different experiences are not necessarily 'job hoppers' who are unreliable or poor performers. The current working culture means that such practices are both common and accepted. With so many choices available, the way people think about work, managing a career, and the role that their job has in their life has changed drastically. Very talented people, confident in their experience and skills, are choosing to engage with top organizations in a different way and on their own terms.

Competition for talent has shifted so that we are not just competing *against* other leading organizations; we are competing *with* the compelling gig economy, which is now attracting talented professionals and motivated subject matter experts who see another option for creating their career path. Have you started leveraging gig workers/consultants to help you achieve business results in a more cost-effective way? Looking at your talent mix is one way to add energy to your culture and get creative about how you engage teams to accomplish great things. Creating a progressive talent strategy today will include a strategy around leveraging this elastic talent and educating managers about the different ways to engage all different kinds of resources to contribute to your culture and your business results. Though incorporating gig workers or consultants into your talent strategy can affect your structure – your career pathing may look different, for example – when integrated correctly, gig workers seamlessly fit into your ideal organizational structure.

In years past, temporary resources were considered 'less desirable', with a lower skill set and mostly thought of for unskilled jobs. Not anymore. Now, these alternative workers are often highly skilled or deeply specialized and are typically high-performing resources. They have chosen to walk away from the traditional 9 to 5 arrangement, walked away from high-paying stable jobs and associated perks, and have made the leap to focus on what they are good at and passionate about. As a forward-thinking and innovative leader, why wouldn't you capitalize on this talent and put their skills to use in your organization? Let's put it this way: if you don't, your competition will.

Companies are figuring out how to engage the many kinds of resources available and it's important to be aware that there may be labour laws that will inform how you need to structure engagements with gig workers, but there are many innovative ways to do so while navigating compliance requirements. Companies who successfully innovate and leverage this new access to highly skilled, variable talent will gain first-mover advantage and will see measurable differences in overhead costs, ability to deliver, and hopefully employee engagement as well.

Bringing it back to culture, it is important to ensure that any resource you consider introducing to your team is going to add something positive. Do not under invest, even in a short-term resource. You need to ensure that the person brings the right attitude and behaviours and is clear about their expectations. All members of the team should have a clear understanding of the cultural norms, what is expected and how they can be part of the culture.

When thinking about talent, do you see how the make-up of a team can look much different from the traditional view? A team can now have full-time permanent employees working alongside highly skilled contingent workers who are all working towards the same business goals. How open are you to embracing this change? To finding the right people to complete the job, project, or task regardless of whether they are your direct hire employee or not? This creative thinking about structure allows organizations to shift to changing business needs and priorities quickly. It creates an agility and adaptability that is greatly needed in our organizations. While this has always been the case, it is even more critical now: COVID-19 is the latest of many developments that have revealed how quickly work can change.

You do not have to wait until you have a new position on your team to start thinking differently about talent. Assess the needs, demographics, and composition of your team today. Have your direct reports start doing the same. Does your current team structure meet the needs of your business today? How about three years from now? Whether a well-established or growing team, it is important to look at how it is designed, how it functions, and honestly examine the skills needed for your business today and in the future.

Leadership expectations and structure

Most organizations have a formal and informal structure. The formal structure is the one written down on paper. This is the one that has levels, departments, and authority channels. The formal structure is what you will generally see on an organizational chart; the informal structure is the undocumented structure and is more about how people interact with one another. To phrase it differently, the former explains how people *should* interact with one another, while the latter often indicates how people actually *do* interact with one another.

> **DEEPER DIVE**
>
> Organizations are now investing in tools that will help them understand some of these informal structures. Organizational Network Analysis (ONA) tools are a relatively new way for companies to take a look at how information flows, who are the critical channels of information, identify people who may be overloaded, and even opportunities to make structural changes to be more effective. ONA tools help you visualize the relationships between people and departments and make it easier to identify any potential barriers to collaboration, communication or information flow that may exist.

At a leadership level, expectations are key to ensuring there is alignment and cohesion between your formal and informal structure. Do you discount certain leaders' opinions when it comes to decision making? On paper, maybe this leader is part of the decision-making chain. Informally, they are left out of the loop, whether due to their lack of ability to effectively make a decision or your lack of ability to address an ongoing performance concern (sorry, we had to go there). While you may think this is isolated or that no one else can see the impact of an ineffective leader, the effects are generally felt throughout the company and often undermine stated efforts of having a high-performing team. Plus, these leaders are often barriers or roadblocks to disseminating critical information elsewhere in the organization. You are working around the issue by not addressing it head on. You are not just hurting your organization, but you are also impacting the leader.

You may think that the leaders themselves do not feel it when they are being marginalized. The truth is, they do feel it and it erodes the trust in the team. How can team members take authority and direction from a leader who doesn't have a valued position with senior figures? This has a further trickle-down effect as the marginalized leader is not leading the team effectively. The tension that this creates is felt at every level and is often the biggest reason that teams, especially leadership teams, are not aligned and moving in the same direction as effectively or efficiently as they could.

The effects of allowing ineffective leadership to stay in place or accepting behaviours that are not aligned with your core values can potentially derail your organization. Having a highly functional, aligned leadership team that leads by example, knows their stuff, and values the responsibilities of leadership as much as their functional responsibilities, is critical to having a successful organization. Effectively stacking the deck, creating a high-functioning team, starts with effective leadership! Take a scan and see if this is working for you.

Remember: the structure is only going to be as successful as the people filling the roles. Often, many leaders think hiring is a job for HR. These leaders should think again.

Whose job is it anyway?

So, whose job is all of this? Candidly, it's *your* job to find the right talent, right place, right time. Regardless if you are a founder, CEO, HR professional, or other executive, it is your job to ensure that your organization can clearly identify talent needs, be innovative and smart about workforce planning, attract the right talent, and be able to motivate and keep them. It is no wonder that for most executives, when asked what keeps them up at night, talent is usually in the top three reasons.

But running out to hire talent to fill an open role is not so simple. It is more than the job description or the structure. You need to think about your organization's values, the specific team's style, your culture today and the culture you want to create and cultivate for the future. It is about being intentional in how you hire and how you structure your organization. It may take time to find the right candidate for you, especially if you are undergoing a transformation and perhaps moving from one type of structure to another. But taking the time to find the right talent is worth it, we promise. Remember, cultures are driven by employees and what each employee brings to work each and every day. The culture will be perpetuated by the structure and each new hire. Rushing into hiring employees because there is an immediate need is a recipe for disaster.

We would be remiss if we did not pause and talk about the HR function briefly. Too often, business leaders underestimate the value and return on investment (ROI) of having a competent, professional, business-oriented HR function. There is a difference between the administrative or compliance functions associated with human resources and the foundational value of organizational design, development, culture, and leadership alignment. Don't wait until you are frustrated with underperformance at a business level or dysfunction within your leadership team to make this area one of the things you manage as actively as you do your strategy and financials. Just as you would not let your executive assistant be your chief financial officer or chief strategy officer, they also should not be your chief human resources officer, chief people officer, or chief talent officer. While you might not yet need a full-time executive dedicated to this function, depending on your business stage and size, invest in a strategic partner to help you get this right from the beginning. There are ways to do this without the cost of a full-time resource that allow you and your organization to benefit from deep experience when you make important structure, people and talent decisions.

As you think about your organizational structure, ask yourself:

- Does your organizational structure today make sense for where you are and where you want to go in the future? If not, why?
- What are the differences between your formal and informal organizational structures?
- When employees leave your organization, do leaders scramble to find a backfill immediately versus taking the time to rethink what they really need?
- How innovative are you willing to get when thinking about talent?
- How intentional is your organization being about having a diverse team?
- Is there healthy discussion at the executive team level to take an enterprise view on talent?
- What is the right talent mix for you given your business model and industry (full-time, part-time, contract, gig, temp, technology)?

Burnout

Before we move on, we want to discuss burnout. Restructuring your organization, redefining roles, breaking down projects into tasks and addressing performance issues on your team all take time. While you may rely on other employees to pick up the work while you transform your organization, do not underestimate the burnout of your top talent.

You may think that waiting to hire a new position or replace someone who left is saving you money without much downside; while that may be true in hard dollar costs, it is certainly far from the truth in other aspects. Your high performers are often the ones who get asked to complete more and more work when you are not properly stacking the team. It really is no surprise that in 42 per cent of organizations, high performers are often less engaged than low performers.[1] To prevent this risky disengagement and burnout, consider hiring highly skilled gig workers on a project-by-project basis. This is especially important if you are going through a restructure and do not want to immediately hire open positions. In this way, with no long-term commitment, you can manage your work, manage the variable costs, and your high performers will feel both valued and respected.

Common pitfalls

In our experience, organizational structure is an area that can be easily overlooked when thinking about culture. When thinking about organizational structure and how to build your team, you must go deeper than the surface and look at old power structures as well. Often, an updated or new structure is added to the old one. This can be like an older home with a brand-new addition that does not quite seem to fit – and before long, cracks begin to appear. We have outlined a few common pitfalls or mistakes to keep in mind when thinking about organizational structure:

The business strategy has changed, but the organizational structure remains the same. As you will see throughout the other areas of organizational culture, when the business strategy changes, elements of the culture must be reviewed. Organizational structure works the same way. Sadly, it is common to see organizations who think they have completely restructured when in fact they have just updated the previous structure. Not updating or trying to slightly restructure with a new business strategy is a recipe for disaster. When your strategy changes, consider starting over with your organizational structure with a fresh set of eyes. Review all facets of the structure, especially the make-up of your team and the power dynamics.

Departments with a long-range focus reporting to departments with a short-range focus. A key example of this is that many organizations have marketing reporting to sales. Sales has a short-term focus – they want to increase sales immediately. They are not playing the long game. Marketing, on the other hand, is about the long-term branding and strategy. By having marketing report to sales, the focus will always be on what marketing needs to accomplish in the short term, perhaps in each sales cycle. This can eventually cause marketing to become more of a sales function and can cause sales to lose sight of both the big picture and need for long-term market positioning and new products. There are many other examples where this can become an obstacle so we recommend that you review your functions, determine which ones have a long-term focus and which ones have a short-term focus, and change the reporting structure to maximize effectiveness and alignment.

Autonomy and control create conflict. Many organizations believe that the organizational structure is either one that has a lot of autonomy, giving employees the authority to make their own decisions, or one in which employees have limited or no authority and the leaders make all of the decisions. The truth is autonomy and control both need to exist in each organizational structure. In fact, departments that are closest to the customer should be given more autonomy because your organization needs sales to be successful. Autonomy does not mean there are no controls in place. It simply means employees have the authority to make decisions, within reasonable boundaries, to benefit the customer and the organization. While autonomy and control do create an inherent conflict or tension, be clear about who has decision-making capabilities and when it becomes necessary to seek approval from leaders.

The right functions have the wrong people working in them. As we've mentioned, every function is made up of a group of activities that it must accomplish. These activities are assigned to various roles and the roles are assigned to various people. For the structure to be effective, the people performing the roles need to be effective. The misalignment between the role and the person trying to fill it can cause the entire structure to collapse. It is like trying to put a square peg into a round hole – it will not work and may create more damage along the way. Be sure to find the right talent for the right role. Again, this may not be full-time employees but highly skilled and specialist gig workers/consultants.

Questions to ask

Knowing when it is time to restructure is important to attracting and retaining the right talent. In the box below, we provide questions to ask yourself to determine whether it is time to restructure.

> **QUESTIONS TO ASK – WHEN IT'S TIME TO RESTRUCTURE**
>
> - How well does our current organizational structure help us achieve our business priorities?
> - Do each of the departments or business units feel like the structure is effective?
> - Are there any unnecessary layers or reporting relationships that do not add value?
> - How effectively is critical information and data provided to the people who need to make decisions?
> - Is it clear who owns the capabilities related to what we need to win in the future?
> - What are the biggest levers for change (process, people, metrics, structure)?

In addition, and as we previously mentioned, if you build it, they will come. The right organizational structure attracts the right level of talent. Below are some questions to ask yourself to determine whether your structure is attracting the right talent.

> **QUESTIONS TO ASK – ENSURING TALENT ALIGNMENT**
>
> - How do we want our employees and leaders to communicate with one another?
> - Are there any employees or leaders we are working around in our structure because they are not in the right role?
> - How equipped are our senior leaders and do they have the right capabilities to support the organization into the future?
> - Are our employees empowered to make decisions and does the structure allow for them to make decisions?
> - What would success look like in terms of business results, in the eyes of the customer, or for your employees?

Moving to action: what you can do next

Here are some actional steps you can take today to ensure your structure is aligned with your business strategies and attracting the right talent. Check back in with these next steps once a quarter or twice a year, at a minimum, to ensure your organizational structure remains efficient and effective:

Review your business strategy. This is really the first place to start to determine whether your structure is aligned with your overarching goals. If you have recently updated your business strategy or had a shift in priorities, think about what your new strategy requires from a people and decision-making perspective. What criteria are most important in a structure to help you achieve your business priorities? Internally, you may notice performance failures, changes in strategy or business model or limitations on new business by the existing structure. Consider changes in not only the internal environment, but the external environment. For example, have there been changes to your customers, relevant technology, the macro-economic situation, regulations, or trade policy that impact your business? Then, after getting clear about the criteria that are important to you, review your organizational structure to see how well it meets those criteria.

Create career-pathing. High-performing talent want to know what their career path may look like with your organization. Be sure your organizational structure is clear as to what the next role is for the employee and what they need to do to move up in the organization. Then, couple this with ensuring you have the right talent development resources to help employees achieve the next level. Before touting your career development opportunities, be sure the resources you have today are in fact effective. Also, be sure all leaders are aware of these resources and who within HR is the best person to speak to.

Identify organizational tensions. With some of your trusted colleagues, work to identify areas within the business where there are current tensions that may be going unaddressed. These usually range from minor (general discord) to significant (personality conflicts and values misalignment) impacting the business. Conducting a review of your organizational landscape regularly will not only present the opportunity for rich discussion and to resolve these potential conflicts as they arise: you may also begin to notice trends that may point to more significant root issues impacting your business. There are often themes in the root causes, with structure and leadership being two of the top root causes we routinely see.

Review organizational levels and spans of control. Often when companies go through growth and change, strong leaders just absorb additional team members, which can result in really large teams that dilute their ability to be effective. Of course, it depends on the function, but for professional-level roles, the best practice is teams of 7–10 per leader. For operational groups like call centres or inside sales, those numbers increase. The opposite can also happen – in an effort to give people career opportunities and have them manage others you will notice pockets of people with only one to two direct reports. This can cause inefficiency and unnecessary levels in your business. While this is good if people really are being groomed for larger roles, it is not helpful if you simply needed to promote them and they are not developing strong leadership skills. All this does is add unnecessary complexity (and cost) to your organizational structure.

Lessons from the real world

What is HR's role in defining the organizational structure?

> Human Resources' role in defining organization structure would be to be a strategic partner with business leaders to develop and deploy a new structure that is better designed to fit the business model. If internal capability does not exist in HR, then hire expert HR consultants as a resource. Either way, to do this, HR partners can assist by leveraging business information related to existing talent capabilities and acquisition of needed talent and assessment. Assessment would include identifying organizational needs to meet business objectives. Included would be an assessment of the current state: highlighting root causes of deficiencies and performance issues; highlighting gaps; sharing best practices to optimize resource allocation and utilization; providing data

on current talent, skills and capabilities and making recommendations to close skills gaps; and input into build/buy decisions for future state organizational design.

Kathy Naylor, Global Human Capital and Business Transformation Adviser and Executive Coach at Change and Leadership Solutions

What is one critical yet often overlooked aspect of organizational structure?

Oftentimes leaders start with looking at the people within their team and trying to fit them into the roles needed, sometimes trying to fit a square peg into a round hole. Instead, I believe it's critical for leaders to first focus on the 'work to be done'. It's always a balance, but I find it's more effective to begin with the work, followed by the knowledge/skills/abilities to do the work, and then fit the people into the equation.

Laurie Robbins Miller, Executive Vice President, Human Resources, Marketing and Communications at Alliance Healthcare Services

The org structure (the hierarchical boxes) is a 'must have' for most organizations, but it only shows part of the picture. Often the structure isn't the problem or the solution. Many times, results are not achieved because of a lack of clarity and accountability for how work gets done. In addition to an org structure, I recommend taking key processes and doing a swim lane diagram to show who does what in the process in the new structure, and also put together a RACI chart so it's clear who is responsible, accountable, consulted, and informed for each important process. This way, people can be held accountable, and rewarded, for their part.

Naomi Werner, Vice President Human Resources at Ossur

Final thoughts

It is important to incorporate your takeaways from this chapter into your action plan. Take a minute and get specific about how these trends and changes in access to talent might be integrated into your business to give you a competitive advantage. Think about your structure today and whether that structure will enable your organization to achieve business results. Hopefully, you identified two or three things that might be low-hanging fruit for opportunity as you read this chapter. Write next steps down and think about how you can partner with your leadership and HR team to implement these changes.

With actionable steps in place to integrate innovative processes, you should feel more open-minded in thinking about talent differently. You have ensured alignment in the leadership team and have everyone rowing in the same direction. There is a clear definition of what it means to be a leader within your company and develop the skills to lead and execute your strategic direction. And you can ensure you have the right HR partners who will focus on creating sustainable systems, deliver value by developing and bringing out the best in your workforce, and ensure you have a partner in your HR team to help you look at the organization.

Now it is time to head into core values.

Endnote

1 Murphy, M (2018) 3 reasons why high performers are often miserable [Blog] *Forbes*, 01 July, https://www.forbes.com/sites/markmurphy/2018/07/01/3-reasons-why-high-performers-are-often-miserable/#179df17d45fc (archived at https://perma.cc/Y7KR-LTFG)

04

Identifying and defining core values

Organizational culture is driven in large part by the company's values, the behaviour of the employees and its business practices. Company values need to be more than words written on the website and hung on the walls of the office. They need to be infused into goal setting, performance reviews, recruiting and training. Our culture has helped us recruit mission-driven employees that are learners and teachers. This has helped us build new products and services faster and gain market share quicker than large banks and other servicers. We have been able to get very large companies to enter into agreements with us when they normally would not have given our size and capitalization.
KEN RUGGIERO, CHAIRMAN AND CEO AT GOAL SOLUTIONS

We have all heard of an organization's MVV (Mission, Vision, Values). The mission defines what an organization does and why it does it. It is the purpose of why the organization exists. The vision is the ideal state, what the organization wants to create. The values define the how – how the business plans to achieve its mission and vision. All are connected, but the values drive the organization forward.

What are core values?

When it comes to business, you probably have an idea for what you value and what you do not. The same goes for relationships and your personal life. Whether you have jotted ideas down, scribbled them on a whiteboard during a brainstorm session, or just kept a running list of words or phrases in your head, chances are you have heard or thought about your values. While our values differ, there are some common ones that we have seen such as integrity, honesty, and collaboration.

But what exactly is a core value? Quite simply, core values are the foundational beliefs of a person or organization. They are the anchors by which people make decisions in and around your company. Scratch that: they are the anchors by which people *should* make decisions in and around your company.

There are different types of core values. There are the general or common *core values*, the deeply ingrained principles that guide behaviours. They are the 'secret sauce' behind a company's culture. An *aspirational core value* is a value the company needs to deliver on its mission and vision, but one that it currently lacks. An example of an aspirational value is innovation in a mature company that needs to deliver new products or services. Finally, there are *accidental core values*. These are the informal values that spontaneously occur over time and eventually just take hold and stay. An example of a positive accidental value is inclusion. While this may not be a formal value of the company, it appears in the organization's behaviours and slowly finds its way into hiring and different Employee Resource Groups (ERGs). Accidental values can also be negative, as in rewarding 'whatever it takes behaviour' even if that behaviour results in backstabbing and lying. Accidental values can be confusing because they are unintentional and therefore not part of the formal core values. For our purposes, we are going to focus on the common definition of core values.

Why are core values important?

Core values not only speak to who you are but to who your company is. They help companies clearly articulate their beliefs and what is meaningful to them, and serve as the guiding principles dictating behaviour.

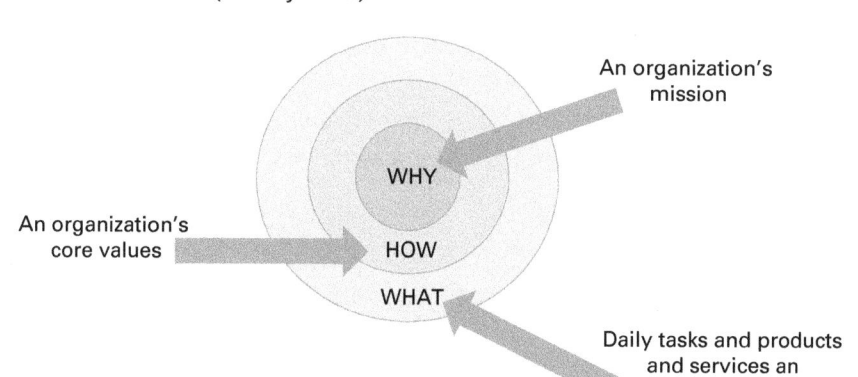

FIGURE 4.1 The Golden Circle Revisited, as adapted from Simon Sinek's The Golden Circle (04 May 2010)

In his famous TEDx Talk, Simon Sinek spoke about The Golden Circle.[1] At the centre of the circle is the WHY. This is the purpose, why do we do what we do. The next level out from the centre is HOW. This is the actual behaviour, how we achieve the WHY. Finally, the outside circle is the WHAT. This is what you do every day to help achieve the WHY. This Golden Circle is applicable to organizations. In Figure 4.1, the WHY becomes the organization's mission, why it exists. The WHAT becomes the daily tasks and products and services an organization sells in order to help it achieve its WHY. The HOW becomes the core values – the behaviours that will help the organization achieve its mission. All three of these circles come together to help form organizational culture. But it is the core values that help provide a moral direction for the culture.

In the past, employees would not pay much attention to an organization's core values. They were more interested in a steady paycheck with a 9 am to 5 pm schedule. Those days are long gone. Employees want to work for organizations that stand for something. They want to be part of a culture where values drive behaviour and are not just random notes in a document or cool wall art. They also want to work for an organization whose values are aligned with their own.

More importantly, core values should not be lip service. Core values should be intentional, and they should be deliberate. As a leader, you need to take ownership of the values and make them the core of your culture. They should not be something that you quickly put together but do not implement. Core values should be infused into *everything* you do, so much so that they are embedded in all aspects of your company's culture, including leadership behaviours. If you recall from Chapter 3, these values should be the first item candidates see to give them insight into your culture by appearing on your job descriptions.

Defining your values

How many organizations have you worked in where the core values were written on the walls? Now how many of those organizations actually lived those values and embedded them into everything they did? The sad truth is, probably not too many. (If the answer is all of them, you have worked for some amazing companies!)

Whether you have created core values, or they need a refresher, there are a few ways to approach this process.

The first step is to get others involved and assemble your team. Yes, you are part of the team. We did not say to hand the process off to your HR department. This is not an HR exercise, just like culture is not something only HR can control. However, you should definitely include members of your executive team, which HR should be part of. If you do not have a formally defined executive team just yet, think about who the leaders are within your organization. Those are the folks you should engage for this exercise. When assembling a team, the important questions to answer are:

- Who really understands the culture we have today?
- Who really understands and knows our employees?
- Who embodies the 'ideal employee'?

Once you have developed a list of the people who you feel would be good to include in the core values team, narrow down the list. You do not want a large group, maybe five to eight leaders and employees. The benefit of having a team is that core values are not articulated from just one person's viewpoint. Instead, they will be a combination of ideas and observations from people throughout the organization (and ideally at different levels) who know the culture well. The reason you do not want to have too large a team is that it can then become difficult to reach consensus and have meaningful dialogue that moves the values forward.

Once a team is assembled, the real work begins. It is time to start collecting data. Start with your core values team. Write down the attributes that made you select each member of the team. Once defined, look at the trends. Are there common attributes that each person has? If so, make note of those. For example, does everyone on the team lead with integrity, regardless of their role or level? Are all employees on the team innovative?

Then, talk to employees who are not part of the core values team. Remember, you are gathering data. While you do not want to define core values by consensus, it is important to involve employees in the process, especially in the early stages before you clearly define any core values.

> **CULTURE QUOTE**
>
> While businesses exist to make money, that should be only one of the driving factors for business leaders. Leaders should start by cultivating meaningful relationships that are rooted in mutual respect. When a business leader first prioritizes the value of team members based on who their people are, rather than what their people do, performance will shoot through the roof because people are working based on relationships. The bottom-line results will follow.
>
> *Dr Anita Polite-Wilson, Founder and CEO at Dr Anita Enterprises, Inc*

Connecting with employees can be done via small focus groups, within teams or, depending on the size of your organization, via various exercises at an all-employee meeting. For the sake of this data-gathering phase, you really want to focus on questions like, 'What's important to us?' 'What makes us uniquely us?' 'What wouldn't we want to change that's special about us as our company evolves?' and perhaps 'Who do we aspire to be?' This last one might apply if you are working through a transformation or significant organizational change.

The goal of these sessions is to extract the essence of your extraordinary culture to define what makes it unique and distinctive. In the box below, we provide the steps of a group facilitation exercise in order to determine core values.

> **GROUP FACILITATION EXERCISE**
>
> - *Set the stage*: Explain what core values are, why they are important and why you are doing them now.
> - *Individual ideas*: Think about the questions outlined previously. Ask people to write down each value they think of on a separate sticky note. Then have each individual put their sticky notes up on the wall.
> - *Grouping*: Ask for volunteers to review the sticky notes and identify themes. This is even better if one of your core values team members can assist. Once the themes are identified, move the sticky notes under each relevant theme so they are grouped together.
> - *Takeaways*: The facilitator should capture the themes, which might be words or phrases, into a master document. Be sure to do this for each session if you hold multiple focus groups.
> - *Consolidation*: Review and consolidate all themes from all sessions.
> - *Roll up*: Review and discuss the consolidated themes with the core values team to further narrow down and make final decisions. Consider if there are themes that are not represented but which are important to the business. During this stage, it can be helpful to engage your marketing department and to think about how the values will be used across the entire employee experience, from recruiting to off-boarding.

If you do not have time for focus groups or an all-employee meeting, send out a survey. Again, it's important to make clear that the survey is not about asking employees to define the values. It is about gathering input to help the core values team define the values. While there are no set questions for the survey, here are some we especially like:

- What draws you to working here?
- What type of culture would you like to see in the office every day?
- What makes our workplace culture unique?
- What type of person do you want to be around every day?
- What type of person do you want to be every day?
- What distinguishes our company from other companies?
- Write a list of words that describe our company. (While not a question, this list provides insight into how employees feel about the company.)
- What do you value in business?
- What do you want customers to know about the organization?
- What do you want potential employees to know about the organization?
- What things would you not want to change about our organization over time?

Also provide at least 10–15 values for people to rank, plus an option to write in any others that come to mind. Remember those common attributes from the core values team? This is a great place to include those common attributes as a starting point. Here are a few to choose from:

- Accountability
- Boldness
- Commitment
- Consistency
- Diversity
- Fun
- Honesty
- Humility
- Innovation
- Integrity
- Joyfulness
- Kindness
- Leadership
- Learning
- Ownership
- Passion
- Quality
- Simplicity
- Teamwork
- Trust

FIGURE 4.2 Core values best practices

WHAT YOU STAND FOR

Describes and lists the basic **values** and **principles** that the organization operates by.

NEEDS TO…

✓ Be clear and simple
✓ Limited to three to seven in total
✓ Define your culture and who you truly are
✓ Be applied to your entire organization

QUESTIONS TO ASK…

✓ What type of culture am I trying to build?
✓ What is the type of person I want to be around every day?
✓ How do I want my customers to feel about my business?
✓ How will I implement each value into the organization?

Figure 4.2 provides a few further items to think about as you talk to employees. These will help provide focus to your input-gathering methods, and so help provide more valuable results.

After talking to others, whether through the survey, focus groups, or an all-employee meeting, start analysing the results as a core values team. Think about trends and patterns. Also take note of any negative themes you may be seeing. While these won't help you define your core values, they will help you in aligning your culture to your core values when it comes time to implement and pull the values through to all aspects of the organization.

Use the data to make a list of 10–12 values that really stand out. As you make this list, think about values through a behavioural, technical and leadership lens. Be sure that the list you are looking at has values that fall into each of these categories. Figure 4.3 provides examples of which values fall into each of these categories.

Belief: Belief is a strong source of energy and motivation. This is what truly drives innovation. The degree to which you believe something is possible is called your 'belief lid'.

FIGURE 4.3 Core values categories

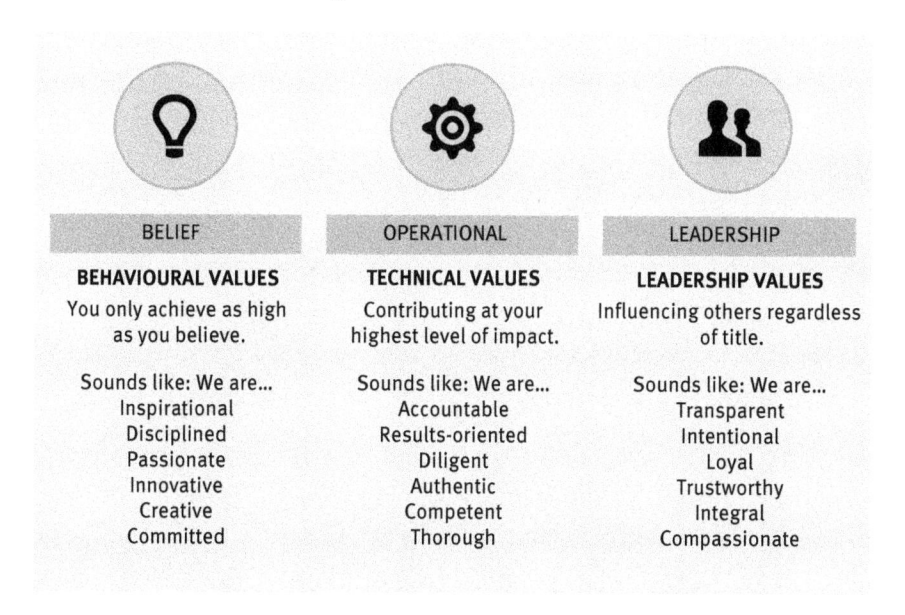

BELIEF	OPERATIONAL	LEADERSHIP
BEHAVIOURAL VALUES	**TECHNICAL VALUES**	**LEADERSHIP VALUES**
You only achieve as high as you believe.	Contributing at your highest level of impact.	Influencing others regardless of title.
Sounds like: We are…	Sounds like: We are…	Sounds like: We are…
Inspirational	Accountable	Transparent
Disciplined	Results-oriented	Intentional
Passionate	Diligent	Loyal
Innovative	Authentic	Trustworthy
Creative	Competent	Integral
Committed	Thorough	Compassionate

Operational: Creating a manageable and repeatable process from best practices will aid in your overall impact. Look at the behaviours of your top performers and their impactful contributions. The level they contribute should become the standard for all employees.

Leadership: When it comes to achieving transformative growth, everything rises and falls on your ability to influence others. All employees, regardless of title, should strive to be leaders.

Once you have your list, start narrowing down the values. One way to do this is to rank the 10–12 you have and then look for common themes. Think about where there is overlap. For example, traits such as 'being proactive' and 'taking initiative' are so similar that they can be consolidated. Remember, having a strong set of core values is about quality, not quantity. You want your values to be meaningful and tangible. Your final list should be around three to seven strong values.

Once you have the list, you need to define the words. This is one of the most important steps, yet many organizations simply do not do it. As an example, ask two different people how they would define 'innovative'. Chances are you will hear two different answers, which leads to two different behaviours, each believing they are being innovative. For example, take the value of 'toe stepping' which we've seen. The intent of the value is to encourage all employees to share their ideas and be open regardless of their level or position within the organization. However, people ended up using this value as an excuse to act like jerks and be disrespectful to others, including their managers. When the value was created, we doubt it was meant to turn into something so negative. This is an example of precisely why we recommend all values having a definition.

Creating concise statements with the value embedded is also beneficial. Below are a few examples of core values with clear definitions:

- Airbnb – Embrace the adventure: We're driven by curiosity, optimism, and the belief that every person can grow.[2]
- Starbucks – Creating a culture of warmth and belonging, where everyone is welcome.[3]
- Adobe – Innovative: We're highly creative and always trying to connect new ideas with business realities.[4]

Just because you have core values does not mean they are interpreted the same by all employees. Even if you have definitions or concise statements, do they leave room for interpretation? Chances are, unless you have clearly defined your values and turned them into *actionable* behaviours, everyone's definitions are going to be slightly different. In order to all row in the same direction, you, as the CEO or head of HR, must clearly define what it means to uphold each value.

Whether you are defining your values for the first time or revisiting them, think about how they will live and show up in your organization. What do the values really mean within your organization? Would everyone on your leadership team interpret them the same way? Would all employees interpret them the same way? Do all employees understand how the values apply to their specific jobs? Do not assume you know the answer to these questions. Ask those on your team and those around you as part of this process.

One example of effectively defining values is Four Seasons Hotels, where Jamie started her HR career. They communicated their values simply in the Golden Rule: to treat others as you would want to be treated. Employees know that if they make a decision that is to the benefit of guest experience, they will be supported. In fact, if they can innovate to go beyond guest expectations, they will be rewarded. This brings empowerment and decision making down to the frontline level. So, whether at the front desk or in housekeeping, employees know how to act in alignment with Four Seasons' values and can feel good about living them.

Once you have narrowed the list with definitions or concise statements, ask yourself: How do these words and statements make me feel? How do they sound when I say them? Do they trigger an emotional response? Then, ask for feedback from employees. Have a focus group or present the values in another all-employee meeting. Your employees need to feel included. These values represent everyone, so everyone should be part of this conversation. We have seen organizations create core values in a vacuum and then leadership was surprised when employees did not feel connected to those values. Remember, your values should be unique to you and help your business stand apart. If you have a value that is generic, such as 'transparency', try to personalize the definition or statement to your organization to make it feel more like your own.

Before deciding on the final list of core values, walk away. Let the words and ideas soak in for a few days, and then revisit them to see if you still feel the same way. Before you ultimately decide, ask yourself:

- How do these words make me feel?
- Are they consistent with who I am and what I want my company to stand for?
- Are any of these words inconsistent with my identity or fundamental beliefs?
- Do they convey the desired level of energy?
- Is there anything materially missing?

Once you finalize the values, plan to roll them out throughout the organization. You want employees to feel comfortable with the values and to really understand them. Ask employees what the values look like, feel like, or sound like to them (trust us, this part is important). Feedback is an essential part of the process and critical for buy-in.

Also, once you have the values defined, you may start to notice behaviours, whether your own or others, that are not aligned with these values and their definitions. You will need to think about how you address these inconsistencies. As we mentioned before, check your own behaviour first. Ensure you are aligned with the values and behaving in a manner that represents them. Next, think about your direct reports. If there is anyone on your team who may not be aligned, do not move to terminate them immediately. Give them a little grace period and explain the meaning and impact of the values. Make it known that you expect all of your leadership team to behave in a manner consistent with these values. Don't just talk the talk. Walk the talk.

Checking in with your values

It is critical to check in with your values after you define them and roll them out. If your organization has had the same values for a while, think about whether they still resonate with you today. How about with your employees? Are the values living and visible with them? Do you and the employees embody the core values in your behaviours? If you said sometimes or not really, you are not alone. According to a Gallup survey, only 27 per cent of US employees surveyed strongly agree that they believe in the values of their organization.[5] Look around your company. That's 27 out of every 100 employees. That means 73 of your employees do not believe in the values. We don't know about you, but that number is startling for us. We all know employees want to work for organizations with a strong set of values, aligned with their own. So, why the significant discrepancy?

Too often, organizations employ a 'set it and forget it' strategy when it comes to values. They set them early when there may be a handful of employees and never revisit them as circumstances change and the organization evolves and grows. While certain values may never change (Integrity, Trust, and Honesty, for example), others may (Innovation, Speed, Cultivate Joy, etc). Think back to Chapter 3 and organizational structure. As your business priorities shift and your priorities change, new behaviours may be necessary. Innovation may be more important than before to achieve success. Change does not mean that your current values go away entirely. They can morph into something more specific. For example, *Cultivate Joy* might become *Be Kind*. A value like *Integrity* might become *Inclusivity*. Allow room for change and growth. As your culture evolves, your values may as well. Values are not meant to be static. Much like your business is dynamic, values are as well.

While it is important to revisit your values, it is equally as important to not break your culture in the process. What we mean by this is you should never start over. When revisiting your values, think about what is working well and which values are still important to you and to the organization. Odds are there are some positive things to your culture, even if you have to dig deep to find those things. Build on what you have created and pivot accordingly, but do not erase all the work that has been done.

There is no formula for when to revisit your values. Some reasons to consider looking at them include growth. If your organization has experienced rapid growth, whether organically or through mergers and acquisitions, it may be time to reassess the new organization that is forming and see whether the same values still apply. A few other reasons to consider checking in with your values include any rapid change in your organization as well as a disconnect with the current values. The biggest reasons a disconnect occurs are due to establishing values without proper input from employees, a lack of leadership support and modelling of the values, and a failure to fully integrate the values in the organization's operating system – the policies, procedures, behaviours and words that collectively create culture.

Bringing your core values to life

The integration of core values into the organization's operating system and employee experience which brings the values to life is one of the most overlooked areas yet is one of the most critical to building a high-performing culture. One of the best ways to bring values to life is to communicate them. This sounds terribly simple and easy to do but many organizations do not do this. Once the values are created, they focus on new hires or external marketing campaigns, leaving the current employees to work things out independently.

Your current employees should know your values. You have spent all of that time coming up with them, so they shouldn't be hollow words updated on a website or painted on the wall. Instead, make it an event. Have a big reveal and really talk about how important the values are to you as a leader, to your executive team and to everyone. Then, spend some time talking about the values and what they mean. It is important for people to know how their personal values connect to the company's core values. Maybe the values are incorporated into a mural on your cafeteria wall so they are front and centre all the time. Or maybe there is a campaign to interview employees who were part of the core values team who came up with the final values. Perhaps you, as a leader, can personalize the values and tell employees why they are important to you and what they mean to you. But, don't stop there.

Core values need to be integrated into company processes, policies, and decision making. You should also take core values into account when looking at your organizational structure. For example, if one of your values is 'own the outcome' your structure should not be mired in layers of leaders and red tape to make a decision. If your value states employees should be accountable for the end-product or result, then you should give them the authority to make decisions aligned with that outcome.

In addition, core values should be used to guide decision making and best practices. Leaders should use the values as a filter to evaluate business practices, asking, 'How does this align with our core values?' Yes, it is hard to keep this top of mind when you have a business to run, but the business will run more smoothly when you practise what you preach and teach.

Let's take performance evaluations as an example. In your current model, are values considered when evaluating performance? If they are not, you may want to consider adding them in.

For one of our clients, we created a matrix performance evaluation system (as seen in Figure 4.4) where employees were evaluated on their objectives (the 'What') as well as the organization's core values (the 'How'). Each were weighed 50/50 as both were considered equally important. The point was to build the values into how employees worked, to make it core to the behaviours and actions they needed to do in order to complete their jobs and work effectively. Imagine the disconnect that can be caused by saying the core values are important to your organization but not holding anyone accountable to upholding them.

Let's say values are already part of your performance evaluation process. Are values also part of how people are compensated? For example, in the example above, someone scoring a 1/4 (1 on the How and 4 on the What) would not receive the same merit increase or year-end bonus as someone scoring a 3/3, furthering the point that values are important. Our client was not only saying they believed the values were important. They were literally putting their money where their mouth was and paying people based on how they embodied the values in their daily jobs.

From a compensation perspective, do you promote employees who are misaligned with the values? Employees may be wonderful at their jobs, completing what needs to get done, but is that more important than how they are completing those tasks? The same goes for increases throughout the year. When considering if someone should receive a raise, do you consider your core values as part of that process? How you compensate employees speaks to what you value as a leader and as an organization. Is there an employee who completes their projects on time and who always meets their objectives, but who does so at the expense of others in a disrespectful way? If you promote this type of employee based only on *what* they do and not also on *how* they do it, then you are not upholding the values of your organization.

FIGURE 4.4 The what and how of performance evaluations

	4	**What:** Exceeds **How:** Does not Meet	4/1	**What:** Exceeds **How:** Partially Meets	4/2	**What:** Exceeds **How:** Meets	4/3	**Exceeds Expectations**	4/4
	3	**What:** Meets **How:** Does not Meet	3/1	**What:** Meets **How:** Partially Meets	3/2	**Meets Expectations**	3/3	**What:** Meets **How:** Exceeds	3/4
Objectives (The "What")	2	**What:** Partially Meets **How:** Does not Meet	2/1	**Partially Meets Expectations**	2/2	**What:** Partially Meets **How:** Meets	2/3	**What:** Partially Meets **How:** Exceeds	2/4
	1	**Does not Meet Expectations**	1/1	**What:** Does not Meet **How:** Partially Meets	1/2	**What:** Does not Meet **How:** Meets	1/3	**What:** Does not Meet **How:** Exceeds	1/4
		1		2		3		4	

Core Values (The "How")

The "What" and the "How" are equally important

What about your rewards and recognition programme? Do you have programmes set up to reward and recognize people for bringing the company's core values to life? We had a client who created a peer recognition programme built around the company's core values. Employees could nominate one another around one of their values. Then, the nomination cards would be displayed publicly so others could see their award. The actual 'award' part was minimal (a gift card and a pin with the value written on it); what was received was much deeper than the items themselves. It was more about living the values and being recognized for doing the right thing. Every action, experience and interaction in your organization should reflect your core values right from day one.

Speaking of day one, when and how do new employees learn about your values? Are they expected to 'pick them up' as they go along? Read them off a plaque on the wall? Instead of leaving this up to chance, incorporate the core values as part of new hire orientation. This way employees are aware of what is expected from day one. From our experience, you should be communicating your core values long before a new employee even sets foot in your office.

Consider how your values show up across the entire employee experience:

> Create awareness → Recruitment → Interviewing → Hiring → Onboarding Engagement → Retention → Offboarding

---

CASE STUDY

Picture this: a high-growth fintech start-up has created a new industry and is currently at 150 employees. They are known to be a great place to work, have inspirational founders, an unparalleled energy, and value people. There is a family feel to the culture and employees have an entrepreneurial spirit. They have forecasted adding 400 employees in one calendar year with limited HR resources to meet the hiring demand. What do you do?

We lived this! While the growth from 10–150 was gradual, the growth from 150–650 was lightning fast. The question we were tasked with answering was,

'How do you grow a company that quickly, maintain the family feel, and still evolve the culture?'

Our answer was simple: you start with the core values, and that is exactly what we did.

To identify core values, you start with the core of the culture. This was not a top-down process or about a few people in a secret room. Rather, we held focus groups throughout the company to hear the voice of all employees who had built the organization and culture. We looked for our core DNA that made us uniquely special, rather than just reaching for something aspirational. This became the pillar on which we built our employer brand.

As recruiters began interviewing candidates, they were able to communicate what it was like to work there, how the role fit into the larger strategic picture, and how the leaders supported the culture. As time went on, we created a Culture Ambassador programme that interviewed candidates not for job/role/knowledge fit, but for core values fit. We were looking for values-aligned talent. We wanted to hire people who were aligned with the values, but who still brought a different viewpoint.

For us, the result of ensuring new hires were aligned to the values was different than if we had looked for a culture fit. The latter can result in 'more of the same'-type thinking and less diversity. The former is more about ensuring how we work and how we make decisions are aligned, even if we come to different final decisions.

In Chapter 6 we will talk a little more about the role values play in attracting and hiring talent. But, before leaving core values, we think it is important to talk about your role as it relates to the values of your organization.

Core values lead to core behaviour

Now that you have spent all that time identifying core values, putting them in place, and examining areas you can incorporate them into as part of your organization's daily practice, let's turn all eyes on you. Are you, as a leader, aligned with your company's core values? We are not talking about believing in your core values but *behaving* in a way that exudes those core values. All the time. Consistently.

Leadership behaviour that is not aligned to your core values is one of the fastest ways to undermine confidence in the leadership team and an effective way to ensure that your top performers leave. Remember, values lose credibility and their meaning becomes hollow when leaders are not walking the talk. Top-down values alignment is essential. You need to know the values, model the values, communicate the values, and celebrate other employees who live those values. Set the right example and set the right tone. Employees are watching you. If you are not modelling the core values, why should they? This is where self-awareness comes back into play. You need to be aware of your own shortcomings and potential misalignment with values. Do you ethically practice your values? If the answer is some of the time or not at all, you need to explore that. This is a time for self-honesty. All too often, leaders do not take the time to examine their own behaviour and amend it to fit the values of the organization. Instead they either feel exempt from having to follow the same cultural norms or they amend the values to better fit with their own behaviour. For example, if there has been a discrimination lawsuit, leaders will add in the value of *Inclusion*. Or if the board of directors is pressuring you as the CEO to deliver, you may want *Urgency* to be a value. Rather than adjusting your values, adjust your behaviours.

Examine your own behaviour before you start scrutinizing and criticizing the behaviour of your executive team. And, if there is a values misalignment on your executive team, resist being the ostrich and burying your head in the sand; even if someone has been a valuable member of the team, you cannot make exceptions to behavioural expectations. Especially at the leadership level! This has to be an area where you do not compromise. You cannot build an exceptional organizational culture and stack the deck in a new way, or in any way for that matter, with leaders who are not aligned with the company values and expectations.

It may seem that when leaders are misaligned with the core values that others can't see it. Trust us: the consequences are felt in the organization and things are way more visible than you think. Everyone is watching executive behaviour and making meaning out of it. Employees can also see how you interact as a team and can sense when there is tension.

You may not want to take action against an executive whose behaviour is not aligned with the values. After all, they could be your head of sales or your COO, right? The truth is, while you may think that keeping them around is helping because of what they 'bring to the table', you're hurting the overall performance of the organization because others see this misaligned behaviour and may mimic it. Additionally, you could be hurting your brand and reputation, both personally and at an organizational level. In turn, this negative reputation will hurt your chances of attracting and retaining top-performing talent, and creating a high-performing culture.

If there is a misalignment of values, you have to move into action and terminate. Period. It is never easy, but the fallout of allowing this behaviour is exponentially worse. In fact, allowing this behaviour has a trickle-down effect that results in poor performance, disengagement and turnover: all the makings of a toxic culture.

Knowing just how bad having an executive that is misaligned with the values can be, are there any conversations that you have been avoiding, but need to have? Whether you answered yes or no, there is always work to be done on ensuring the organization's core values exist, are relevant, and live in all aspects of your culture.

Common pitfalls

From our experience, the values exercise, and the process of identifying your core values for the first time or revisiting them to make sure they are still relevant, is a prime example of intent versus impact. While you may have the best intentions of wanting to create a culture built on a solid foundation of core values, the actual result is that your net impact may fall far short and not leave a lasting or significant impact at all. Here are a few common pitfalls to look out for when identifying, defining, and re-evaluating your core values:

The values are too closely tied to the founder. It is hard not to feel protective of the organization, the people and the culture you've built when you're a founder. This is your baby, after all. However, designing your core values around a founder's life philosophy can be problematic. For example, there is an inherent implication that the founder will have the final say. If the organization and the employees are supposed to think and behave like the founder, then, by default, whatever the founder does or says is always correct. The organization is a collective of different people with diverse backgrounds and experiences that all come together to create culture. It should go without saying that your values should be representative of this diversity and should be objective.

The values are not authentic to your organization. Employees can spot inauthentic values quite easily. This can often be the outcome when executives create the values in a bubble without understanding the behaviours that are actually occurring today within your culture. For example, adding *Communication* as one of your values because 'it sounded good' is not a reason to add it, especially if your organization is terrible at communicating! The values should mean something to your organization today and should not be a marketing or public relations gimmick.

Overlooking values contradictions. Inherent tension is caused when you have two seemingly contradictory values. How can you move fast and provide a high level of quality at all times? This can leave employees scratching their heads. These contradictions are okay to have, you just need to explain them. Employees will not embody all your values all the time. Instead, provide examples of how they can minimize this tension. For example, moving fast may be about moving forward and gaining momentum while a high level of quality is about the service provided to customers and other stakeholders. Whatever your contradictory values, be sure you give employees clear guidance on how best to exhibit each. This is also where prioritizing values can be helpful. Perhaps in this case, quality would trump moving fast.

More is not always better. Values should not be a laundry list of words, even if they do apply to your culture or the culture you want to create. It is easy to get caught up in words that sound great, but how important are they to your culture? When it comes to values, more is not always better and focusing on a few strong, meaningful values will go a long way.

Questions to ask

As we previously mentioned, core values need to guide how employees work and behave. The box below provides questions to ask yourself to determine whether your values are making the desired impact.

> **QUESTIONS TO ASK – ASSESSING CORE VALUES**
>
> - Do our values speak to what is most important to our organization?
> - Do our values help guide decision making in both good and bad times?
> - Are our high performers living our values on a consistent basis?
> - Do I and the leadership team consistently model the values?
> - Are our values helping create a high-performing culture that is attracting and retaining top talent?
> - What about these core values are unique to us?
> - Are these core values too generic so that they could apply to any company?
> - Are our core values the same or similar to those of our competitors?

In addition to assessing your core values, you need to ensure they are integrated into all aspects of your culture, including your HR and business strategy. In the box below, we have provided some questions to ask yourself to ensure your values are embedded appropriately.

> **QUESTIONS TO ASK – INTEGRATING CORE VALUES**
>
> - Do we reward employees for exhibiting our core values? For example, do we reward the desired behaviours?
> - Do we reward employees even if their behaviour is not aligned with our values? For example, do we reward bad behaviours, even unintentionally?
> - How are our core values exhibited in our Leave of Absence policy?
> - How are our core values modelled in each area of our employee experience?

- Can new employees clearly articulate our values and what they mean?
- Do the careers page on our website and our job descriptions clearly list our values and how they differentiate us from our competitors?
- What expectations have we set for leaders to publicly demonstrate our core values?
- If I ask people from around the company to name our core values, can they?
- Do the values have consistent definitions for what they mean?
- Are there any company rituals that we can start to help us reinforce the core values? For example, should we have leaders start each internal meeting with the team naming the core values?

Moving to action: what you can do next

Below are some actionable steps you can take today to ensure your values are aligned to the culture you want to create and are lived throughout your organization on a daily basis. Come back to these next steps frequently to ensure you are making progress and moving in the right direction.

Conduct a self-audit. How aligned are your personal values to those of the organization? That's not a rhetorical question. Take an honest look. Where are the gaps and why do they exist? As a CEO or HR leader, you need to be the embodiment of the values. Your organization's values must be aligned with your own values. This alignment allows us to connect to our work in a more meaningful way, allowing us to be more effective at our jobs – more effective at leading the organization. In addition, this alignment leads to more authenticity. You are not putting on a show when you are in the office. You actually believe in the values and live them.

Check in with the organization's values. Are employees living the values? If you are not sure how to answer that question, then you need to start walking around and visiting your employees. In the age of more remote or virtual work, this can be difficult, but still doable.

Set up one-on-one meetings with team leaders. Have them walk you through a process or what their department is currently working on. Look for things that are going right. Ask questions around things you do not understand. Ask how their employees are doing, how they feel about the values. This is your chance to stay connected and talk with the people who are doing the work to see how the values actually live in your company. This is also a great opportunity to show how aligned you are with the values as well.

Consider getting an outsider's view. It can be hard for us to see our organization and our values as they really are versus through our lens of being in the same environment every day. Sometimes, we need an external viewpoint to help us gauge whether our values are really accurate and whether leaders are truly aligned. The point of this external lens is to provide clarity and an honest, unbiased look into what is actually happening and not just what we think is happening. This outside perspective can help us gain awareness and realign our efforts to ensure what we are saying is important is also accurately reflected in what we are doing.

Take a leadership inventory. Determine whether the behaviours of each executive are consistently aligned with the core values. If they are not, determine how you can either course correct their behaviour or work to move them out of the organization – something we call External Mobility. Remember, no matter how brilliant someone's work is, certain behaviours create a toxic culture. Your leaders should be doing this on their teams as well. However, when it comes to values, start at the top first and then work your way down into the organization.

Lessons from the real world

Why are core values so important to organizational culture?

> Any organization has values. Sometimes you don't know what they are, or there are as many values as there are people in the organization. Many organizations state them on a wall somewhere. The point is

whether the values, whatever they are, are shared. If they are, then the organization can move in any chosen direction. If they are not, you've got a Roman galley with no drummer. And any value that exists which causes people to more likely behave in congruence with it is a 'core' value. There is no such thing as 'non-core' values. Those would be values that shift with the moment, often used as justifications to do whatever one wants in that moment.

Stan Sewitch, Vice President, Global Organization Development at WD-40 Company

Final thoughts

If done correctly, core values serve as anchors for your culture. Think of culture like a house. The core values are the foundation upon which the rest of the house will be built. If there is a crack in the foundation, then the walls could come crashing down. Rather than patching the cracks, work to fix the root cause, re-securing the house to a strong base.

Before moving on, take a few minutes to write down two or three key takeaways from this chapter with regards to your organizational core values. Think about aspects of the values that may be working well and areas which could use some attention. Now, looking at that list, next to each takeaway write down one action item that you will commit to doing to ensure your foundation stays strong.

What did you commit to do?

Endnotes

1 Simon Sinek (2010) TEDxPuget Sound – How great leaders inspire action (video) https://www.ted.com/talks/simon_sinek_how_great_leaders_inspire_action?language=en (archived at https://perma.cc/FX62-5QX5)
2 https://careers.airbnb.com/ (archived at https://perma.cc/Z8WF-QP43)

3 https://www.starbucks.com/careers/working-at-starbucks/culture-and-values (archived at https://perma.cc/A4ZJ-KL4D)
4 https://www.adobe.com/about-adobe/fast-facts.html (archived at https://perma.cc/QV2B-7B3P)
5 Dvorak, N and Nelson, B (2016) Few employees believe in their company's values, *Gallup Business Journal*, 13 September, https://news.gallup.com/businessjournal/195491/few-employees-believe-company-values.aspx (archived at https://perma.cc/L5XH-N8YA)

05

Skills for now and the future

Approach the work of culture building with a sense of servant leadership – eg don't ask others to do things you wouldn't do yourself, be willing to take feedback and learn from everyone on your staff, and engage with authenticity; this means owning the fact that you are human and may have the best of intentions but will make mistakes. Servant leadership builds strength as it encourages employees to invest themselves in the work, it creates a space where failure is ok as long as you learn from it, and helps to surface good ideas from across the organization.

BROOKE VALLE, CHIEF STRATEGY AND INNOVATION OFFICER AT SAN DIEGO WORKFORCE PARTNERSHIP

Everyone possesses a particular set of skills. Maybe you are a natural born leader. Maybe you are the top salesperson on your team. Maybe your talents shine more behind the scenes. Whatever your skill set, they can be translated into what we refer to as key competencies, which are specific desired employee qualities, traits, or behaviours.

Think about your rockstar employees. What makes them so amazing? Their 'do whatever it takes' attitude? Their technical knowledge of your product or service? Their ability to consistently meet deadlines? Why are they considered your 'go to' employee when you have an issue or a new project?

Now, what separates these employees from the rest of the pack? If the rest of your employees are 'great' but do not possess the key traits necessary to take your business into the future, then your business will not have a future. We are not saying that all employees need to have the exact same set of qualities or traits. However, there should be some foundational competencies that all employees possess, even in differing amounts.

Before you can assess your employees, though, you need to clearly define your top key competencies among an ever-changing business landscape. While there are endless desired traits or qualities, we have narrowed it down to 12 core competencies that are pivotal in our ever-evolving work environment for all employees to possess:

1 *Adaptability: The ability to embrace change.*
   If a common phrase within your organization is something like, 'that's just how we've always done it', then your employees are probably not highly adaptable. Technology is evolving so quickly that the outdated tasks we used to do manually no longer exist. The rate at which we can complete certain projects is faster than it has ever been. In order to embrace change, create opportunities for your workforce to become more adaptable by exposing them to new tasks. For example, do a rotation where someone from marketing spends time in finance, or someone from sales spends time in product. Consistently ask your team to step outside their comfort zone to flex that adaptability muscle. Adaptability actually increases productivity as well. Imagine if the time employees felt stressed due to a change was used instead to flex and handle the change?

2 *Workplace agility: The ability and willingness to learn from experience and then apply that knowledge.*
   We hear the word agile used in technology a lot, but the concept can be applied across the organization too. The consistent need to act quickly and make fast decisions is evident now more than ever. The ability to change also leads to increased productivity and higher-performing teams. It is not just the ability to change quickly that matters; it is also about the ability to work together more

cohesively as one team. Agility leads to fast thinking and quick decision making. Your organizational structure will affect how agile your organization is. So, if you are thinking about agility as one of your key competencies, consider whether the organizational structure supports it.

3 *Critical thinking: The ability to objectively analyse a concept or scenario.*
When you are a critical thinker, you consider all the facts and differing opinions/sides/viewpoints and come to a sound and logical conclusion. By nature, we make decisions without thinking 'critically'. We make judgements based on personal opinions, biases, and emotions. Those judgements lead to decisions. Critical thinking is about being intentional and putting your own biases aside. In doing so, you can be more creative and more effective at work. Critical thinking is important as it allows teams to effectively diagnose problems together, identify possible solutions and resolve any conflicts that may occur. Possessing the ability to be a critical thinker increases self-awareness as well. Critical thinkers see challenges from multiple points of view, minimizing their need to perpetually defend their own personal beliefs.

4 *Emotional intelligence: The ability to recognize emotions and adjust thinking and behaviour accordingly.*
You might know someone who can 'read a room' or seems intensely self-aware while also being able to understand and interact well with others. These people value emotional intelligence and use it as an asset both in life and in business. We previously talked about self-awareness in reference to leadership; emotional intelligence relates to a person's ability to regulate themselves and adjust to those around them. Often, people who are strong in this area will be viewed as valuing continuous learning and investing time and effort into their own and others' development.

5 *Cultural intelligence: The ability to understand, respect and work with people from diverse backgrounds, races, genders, etc.*
Diversity, inclusion, and belonging is critical to designing an exceptional organizational culture, as we will cover in Chapter 9.

Possessing cultural intelligence allows employees to adapt to different perspectives with the understanding that these differing viewpoints add to the culture and organization rather than detracting from it. In addition, this understanding and awareness aids in communication, another important core competency mentioned later in this list.

6 *Customer focus: The ability to ask questions and get feedback from internal and external customers to improve products and processes.*
One of the most important rules in business is to know your customer and put them at the centre of everything you do. 'Customer' can mean both internal and external stakeholders. Creating a customer focus allows room for change, adaptation, and the opportunity for your organization to shape a strategy with the customer in mind. Customer focus is also about building relationships with your customers and listening to and incorporating any feedback they may have into your future products and services. It can be difficult for people who are not self-aware to have a customer focus. This occurs because it can often be difficult for these people to ask for feedback and listen for areas of opportunity. Also, consider whether your core values consist of a customer focus, especially in service-based industries.

7 *Tech savviness: The ability to understand and work with the various technological advancements.*
We are in the middle of the 4th Industrial Revolution. Unlike those before, this revolution is characterized by the introduction of major technology, including artificial intelligence (AI), big data and extended reality. While employees do not need to be familiar with all the various technologies that exist, they should be comfortable working in an environment consisting of these technologies. Additionally, employees should be aware of how various platforms could affect their job as well as the business. Being tech savvy is also about adapting to and learning new technologies that your organization may introduce. For example, project management software versus excel to keep track of large projects and report out in a consistent manner.

8 *Collaboration: The ability to work with others to deliver a result.*
Collaboration is critical. It may look very different in today's world of remote work and global teams, but the strength here is when people prioritize decisions that are best at a company level, not a project or department level, collaborate and innovate across business functions, and incentivize teamwork over individual success. For collaboration to be successful, individuals need to possess interpersonal skills, strong communication skills and be open to knowledge sharing. When thinking about collaboration think about your organizational structure. Does is support a collaborative environment?

9 *Communication: The ability to give and receive direct feedback.*
Communication is key, but it is not always easy to communicate with authenticity and transparency or to share information openly. Consider various ways of communication in order to be sure that you are connecting with people in multiple fashions. Start by listening, asking questions, and modelling the communication you would like to see. Consistently seek input from people across geographies, cultures, and backgrounds across your company.

10 *Ownership: The ability to hold accountability for yourself and others.*
Ownership is one of the most important components of building trust. Do what you say you are going to do... consistently. Take ownership for problems and demonstrate the initiative to solve them, even if you did not create them. Hold others accountable for what they are responsible for. Model the behaviours you expect from others. All employees should be invested in the organization and the eventual outcome of the decisions they make and the work they do. By taking ownership, decisions can be made quicker and problems can be resolved faster.

11 *Design thinking: The ability to develop processes based on a desired outcome.*
In recent years, design thinking has become extremely popular. Initially used to create or improve on products or services with the customer in mind, design thinking is now being used internally with the employees as the customer. Think of design thinking

as a defined process for creative problem solving. An example of design thinking is, as a leader, thinking about the type of organization you want to create. Using that as the desired outcome, you work backwards. Areas you think about are understanding your end-user and what they need, clearly defining those needs and the problems, using both of these to start creating ideas and thinking outside of the box as to how you're going to achieve your desired state. This stage is all about brainstorming. Then you're going to start creating the solutions and experimenting with them. For culture, this is where focus groups help. You will then test your solutions. These steps do not have to be completed in sequential order. Employees should also take this approach in their daily jobs, thinking about what they want the outcome to be and how to achieve it.

12 *Entrepreneurial mindset: The ability to identify and capitalize on opportunities, learn and move forward from setbacks and succeed in a variety of environments.*

You do not need to be an entrepreneur to think like one. However, employees who possess an entrepreneurial mindset can easily identify various opportunities, whether internal or external, and capitalize on them. When they encounter setbacks, they are not derailed but rather use these setbacks as learning opportunities and move forward. Employees who possess this competency can overcome obstacles by thinking creatively. Plus, if employees approach their role as if they are running their company, they are more invested in the outcome.

CULTURE QUOTE

For CHROs or CEOs, build a robust employee communication function – it is so important in today's information overload to be out front and provide consistent messaging. Communicate, communicate, communicate. Communicate changes ahead of time. Employees want and seek leadership in times of change, and although they may not like the message, in general they will respect and appreciate it. If you

> proactively communicate then you can feel better that you did your best. Be transparent as much as possible – even past your comfort level. This treats employees as adults and the professionals you expect them to be, and over 95 per cent will act like it. If you are not transparent, the bad part of human nature will take over and bring out the worst. People will make things up to fill in the unknown.
>
> Steve Weiss, Director of Compensation at Mitchell International

While all employees should exhibit some or all of your core competencies, leaders should possess a few more.

1 *Execution: The ability to act.*
It's easy to talk strategy, make plans, and sit around dissecting your business or consuming more information instead of taking action. As a leader, you must be able to execute. While it is important to be strategic in your role and to think critically, it is equally important, if not more so, to act. Have a vision and then execute. It is only through action that you can see what works and what does not. Balance execution with information and data gathering, but do not let too much information cause you to have analysis paralysis and prevent you from executing.

2 *Crisis management: The ability to recognize, identify, and respond to threats with self-awareness and relationship management.*
In light of the COVID-19 pandemic, we all learned it is crucial for leaders to not only protect revenue but also maintain a strong culture in the face of a crisis. We now know how vital it is to plan ahead, to be able to pivot, and not panic. Crisis management is not about having all of the answers, but it is about relying on your resources and other leaders to help guide you.

CASE STUDY

Take Gravity CEO, Dan Price. Gravity Payments is a company that helps small businesses process payments. As their clients started to see a decrease in business and revenue to the tune of 55 per cent, Gravity was faced with a decision: lay off 20 per cent of the workforce or go bankrupt. Neither option was acceptable to Price, who decided to enter crisis management mode and take action in a thoughtful way. He held a town hall meeting where he explained the situation to all employees. He then held a series of smaller focus groups with his COO asking employees for their thoughts and their opinions on what Gravity should do. Some employees could not take a pay cut because they had a new mortgage or a new baby. So, it was not an option for Price to cut pay across the board either, but all employees wanted to help and contribute. The final solution was to have employees anonymously provide how much they could cut their pay by. Those who earned more could give back more.[1] Those who earned less, gave what they could. All in all, everyone gave something.

---

3 *Social intelligence: The ability to know yourself as well as others.*
Self-awareness, as we talked about in Chapter 2, is a component of social intelligence. However, social intelligence is broader and encompasses understanding the dynamics of social situations and the ability to effectively navigate in those social situations. Leaders need to know when to speak, when to listen, what to do and what to say. Taking cues from the surroundings is essential to social intelligence. We have all seen, or at least known of, leaders who may tell a funny joke, but the timing is all wrong. Or of leaders who seem uninterested in meeting someone new. Social intelligence in leadership leads to better communication and a high-performing team, especially because others are looking to the leader for their own social cues.

4 *Negotiation: The ability to effectively influence others.*
Leadership is about influence and the ability to sway perception or change minds while maintaining relationships. The power to effectively negotiate is important today and will continue to be important into the future considering there are more outside influences and technological advancements affecting businesses. In addition, the ability to influence will remain crucial to selling your vision to your team and those who need to be bought in.

5 *Anticipate change: The ability to have strategic foresight to see change.*
Anticipating change is not about having a crystal ball where you can see into the future. As we've mentioned, advances in technology

are creating change at a rapid pace. Leaders need to be ready to anticipate those changes and be first movers with the ability to create change before the change is forced on them. It is the difference between being proactive versus reactive; between having a say in the change versus change happening to you. Leaders need to have a future focus in order to anticipate change. Anticipating change is also part of crisis management.

We know there are many more core competencies that employees and leaders need to possess. However, the ones we have mentioned we believe are fundamental to how work is changing. Additionally, all will play key roles in an organization's culture. Knowing your core competencies helps shape how you hire, who you hire, what rewards you offer and so much more. As we have seen with the COVID-19 pandemic, how we work is changing rapidly, with a significant shift to a virtual or remote environment. The competencies mentioned above allow employees and leaders to adapt to these changes efficiently and effectively without losing sight of the overarching business goals.

Natural born leaders?

Now that we have identified some top key competencies, let's ask the big question: are you born with these competencies or can they be developed? The quick answer is both.

While some people are born with a 'go-getter' attitude and already possess an affinity towards leadership and the necessary skills required, some grow into it. Think back to when you were a child. Was there another child in the playground who was clearly the leader of the group? The one that other kids wanted to follow and emulate? Perhaps you were that leader. Or perhaps you wanted to be that leader or were more comfortable in the crowd. Regardless, we think of leaders today as people who possess the necessary skills needed for achieving high performance and business success, especially when they have the right attitude.

Before you get down on yourself for not being a childhood leader, the truth is that only about 30 per cent of leadership skills are genetic.[2] This leaves the door wide open for the ability to learn new skills. Since leadership is a personal journey, it boils down to your willingness to be taught and acquire new leadership skills.

We have all seen people who were promoted into leadership positions because they were amazing at their individual contributor jobs and exhibited great competency. Decision makers think that because they were *good* at their job, they would in turn make great leaders. This is far from the truth. Some of these individual contributors do not want to be managers. And others may not possess the skill set necessary. This can lead to a feeling of being overwhelmed and underprepared when promoted, which can lead to underperformance. Not to mention it can be uncomfortable to suddenly oversee other people. But this is precisely when being open to learning new skills is key. If these new managers are open to learning new skills, then they can turn into good leaders.

It is also important to remember that people learn in lots of different ways and especially mirror back what is modelled. If you work to ensure that every person put into management prioritizes the portion of their job related to developing, leading, and managing people, then you set the expectation for everyone who considers accepting that responsibility. Here, organizational structure, especially spans and layers, is critical. Think about how many employees each leader must manage. As we previously mentioned, 7–10 direct reports are optimal, allowing leaders to develop their people. Also, think about what you expect from your leaders with regards to the technical aspect of their role. How much of their time can they dedicate to coaching, leading, and developing their employees and how much of their time do they need to dedicate to other work and tasks they need to accomplish?

Some organizations are large enough to build out manager development or emerging leader programmes internally that create a specific curriculum to teach the fundamentals of what it means to be a leader in that organization. Others leverage external development programmes. Either way, consider investing in formal development opportunities for people who move or are on the path to move into leadership roles. Also consider your core values and the key competencies in these training and development programmes. Whether you create your own programmes or partner with an external vendor, be sure your values are at the centre of the curriculum.

Remember: leadership can be taught, but it takes prioritizing it as part of your culture for people to invest their time and energy into building these skills.

Customizing competencies

While the skills we have mentioned are what *we* think are important for organizations to look for now and into the future, it is also important to think about your specific organization. For example, at a start-up biotech company Hema used to work for, adaptability, agility, and execution were in high demand. The organization needed these skills because they were a lean organization with not a lot of employees early on. Think of an 'all hands on deck' scenario.

Everyone was expected to contribute and be cross-functional. As the organization grew, HR was better able to align the specific skills needed with the organization's short- and long-term objectives. As this started to happen, employees with specific skills needed to achieve those objectives were moved into centres of excellence to focus on their jobs. Hiring was geared towards the specific skills and less on a 'jack of all trades' mentality. As organizations become more established, they have a better idea of what they need. This was not the case when Hema first started at this organization, but it certainly was the case a few years later.

The example above showcases that as organizations evolve, what is required from employees also evolves. This is a natural evolution and happens at different stages of the organization's lifecycle, but if you have hired the right behaviours and leadership competencies, then people can adjust much more easily. In fact, you may even find that employees are hungry for this clarity. However, if you have the wrong behaviours, it is easy to find yourself having to make difficult changes as people can't flex as the organizational needs do.

The most important element, regardless of stage, is to ensure the skills you are identifying are in fact important to your organization and are necessary to achieve your corporate objectives and strategy. Customize these competencies and worry less about what skills your competitors require. Instead, focus on your organization and creating a skills bank that will help you achieve success.

This process begins with identifying behavioural competencies required from employees (new or current) at the current stage of your business (ie flexibility, utility players, willing to do whatever it takes) who will be able to meet future needs. Regardless of the stage of your company, linking the core competencies to the business strategy is crucial for success. Training or hiring specific competencies that are irrelevant to your business is a waste of time and money, not to mention that it can result in disengaged employees. To link competencies to your business strategy, think about the major themes or core competencies required to achieve your business strategy. For example, if a key corporate objective is to create two new products in the next five years, then perhaps innovation is going to be important. If, on the other hand, automation and technology are going to be key business priorities, perhaps tech savviness is a needed key competency. Once you have the central themes, ie innovation, think about the specific behaviours needed to achieve success. Perhaps with innovation this looks something like agility and collaboration.

Partner with HR to help identify these core competencies and behaviours. Once identified and defined, ensure there is alignment at the executive level, then use these competencies to hire new employees and train existing employees.

Develop the team internally while simultaneously building it out and bringing new workers on board who possess the competencies you are looking for. If you do not spend time on the internal team, then adding people to the team who possess these skills will cause friction. The idea is to keep talent, not drive it away! (More on this in Chapters 6 and 7, by the way.) Also, be sure that your management and employee development programmes we mentioned above are updated to reflect these key competencies. Much like the core values, embed these competencies into everything you do. Let's come back to this in a moment.

Consistency is key

As you start training employees in the new competencies and hiring employees who exhibit the competencies you need moving forward, you need to be sure to be consistent, especially at the leadership level with the leadership competencies. For instance, do you have a consistent standard of what leadership means and looks like across your leadership team? Does the leadership team have the skills necessary to manage the people and the organizational aspects of the business? This cannot fall on the shoulders of one HR or talent leader. It also cannot be enough to identify the skills necessary. It becomes more about how you are going to ensure your employees and your leaders have those necessary skills. Above, we provided only five of the countless leadership competencies that exist. Much like the core competencies for all employees, make sure your leadership competencies speak to who you are.

As your business grows, you must be willing to take an honest look at your leadership team and the competencies and behaviours they possess. This is a common challenge for growing start-ups that are the last to recognize when they need to add management structure and enterprise-level skills. It can also be difficult to part with leaders who may have helped build the infrastructure early on, but simply do not possess the skills to scale the organization. This is a common situation we see with many of our start-up clients. We often help these organizations transition these leaders and hire someone who does possess the necessary skills for the next stage in the company's evolution.

Infusing core competencies

As mentioned, it is not enough to identify core competencies and then hire or train to them. You also need to infuse these competencies into your performance evaluation process. How well are employees performing at these competencies? For example, if customer focus is a core competency, you should be evaluating your employees and leaders on it. Remember, a customer can be internal or external, so departments such as accounting and HR can also be evaluated on this. While we have focused on core competencies so far, job competencies are also an important part of performance management. Job competencies are the specific skills necessary to perform a certain job. Both types of competencies are needed to be successful. Job competencies are extremely specific to the organization and the role being performed. Core competencies are much broader than one particular job or role and can be applied in a multitude of settings across the organization.

Assessing performance based on competencies requires introspection and the ability to comprehensively look at all measures of performance. It also allows managers to determine if additional training may be needed and, if so, where that training should focus – core or job-related competencies. Communication is more open in these types of reviews and performance plans are more holistic.

Core competencies revisited

Just like your organization evolves, core competencies evolve, as we have mentioned. Do not forget to check in with your competencies to see if they are still applicable to your organization. How often should you check in with your identified skills? The answer is it depends. If there is a change in business priorities or strategy, you should definitely review the competencies to see if they still apply. This is also a good time to see if there are some competencies that are more important than others. For example, social and emotional intelligence may be at the top of the list, along with cultural intelligence, during the time of COVID-19, as many employees are working remotely. Another time to check in with your competencies is if the business has undergone a massive shift, such as a recent merger or acquisition.

Partner closely with HR to establish a review cadence that works for your organization. Be sure this review consists of both soft skills as well as technical competencies.

Welcome to the dark side

While we have been talking about competencies, also consider the strengths that employees and leaders need to possess. It's important to remember that every strength, when overused, has a dark side. For example, high performers tend to be adaptable. They have the ability to 'go with the flow' or be flexible and change course as needed to keep a project moving. However, if an employee is *too* adaptable, they may be viewed as too easily accepting of change without questioning the *need* for change and this can lead to a lack of direction or execution.

We have already discussed the advantages of critical thinking, right? This is necessary at all levels of the organization and especially with an increase in responsibility and leadership. But when overused, critical thinking can be a roadblock to finishing a project and can be seen as slowing down the process when time is of the essence.

This is why it is so important to clearly define the skills and competencies and then directly connect them back to the job. In effect, you are setting some guardrails so employees do not blur the line and move into the dark side.

> QUESTIONS TO ASK TO CREATE A BLUEPRINT FOR YOUR KEY SKILLS AND COMPETENCIES
>
> - What skills have you hired for in the past? Which of these skills still apply to your business today? *This will help determine what skills are relevant for your organization.*
> - What technical skills are necessary for employees to possess based on your organization's industry and roadmap? *This will help determine any unique skills, either for your industry or your organization, and whether these skills are hard to find.*
> - Do all employees need to possess these technical skills? If not, which employees need them? *This is helpful as you start to write job descriptions and interview candidates.*
> - How long have you been in business? Are you still in growth mode or are you now sustaining? *This will help determine whether agility and adaptability are at the top of your list or whether they are further down.*

- Do employees work mainly in teams where there is a high need to communicate or are individuals autonomous? *This will help determine whether teamwork is a skill high on the list.*
- Who is expected to execute on ideas or create strategy? *This will help determine how much execution vs strategy skills employees will need; this could be higher the higher you go in the organization.*
- What makes your organization unique? *This is generally helpful as you determine if there are skills or attributes that set your organization apart from others.*
- Do you have a call centre? *This will help determine the degree to which customer service is a needed skill.*

Common pitfalls

Most leaders are moving fast, responding to issues as they arise and dealing with the most urgent needs. Here are some common pitfalls to keep an eye out for:

Failing to clearly define the role of leadership. We have all seen the best salesperson or smartest engineer promoted to manager. Do not fall into this mistake of putting someone into a leadership role who may or may not have the interest and skills to be successful. Taking your best-performing technical person and making them your worst-performing leader is not a successful strategy. Think about your leadership competencies. Does your star individual contributor possess these leadership competencies? Is there a training and development programme they can attend to help them develop the necessary skills? Above all else, do they want to be in a people management role?

Looking too near term. We often find that too many leaders have an internal focus and are not keeping an eye on external trends. Often when the need for new skill sets and capabilities to deliver on strategies is most urgent, you will either struggle to find them or have to overpay in the market. If you plan ahead, you have more choices around whether you should 'build/develop' or 'buy' the skills needed. When you plan in advance, you can be more strategic about filling those needs and not simply reacting to the current issue or problem.

Forgetting to update the skills needed to deliver when there is a change in strategy. We often say your talent, culture, and organization need to be as actively managed as your strategy and financial performance. We know most leadership teams make the time to conduct strategy sessions and create business plans. In fact, most if not all leadership teams dedicate multiple days to this at offsite locations. However, too often leaders skip the step of ensuring that the organization has or will have the skills necessary to deliver on that carefully crafted strategy. Do not take it for granted. Work to incorporate the skills and the necessary updating of skills into the strategy itself. Make it part of the process. Then, take it one step further. If you need new skills, how should you obtain the new skills? Should you build the talent internally by identifying people with the interest and ability to learn the required skills and either have them learn from others, identify training opportunities (internal or external), or get them formal education? Or should you consider getting the talent externally? You will need to assess the timing of when the skills are needed based on your strategy and priorities. These questions will help you determine if you need to hire a full-time resource to join the team for the long haul or if you can augment the team with elastic talent to quickly deliver on specific needs. This is a great place to think about talent differently!

Questions to ask

We've talked about how to ensure you are assessing and planning so that your organization has the necessary skills to deliver on your business strategy. Below, we provide questions to ask yourself and your team to ensure you are well positioned for success.

QUESTIONS TO ASK – SKILLS NOW AND IN THE FUTURE

- What are our key areas of focus?
- What are the critical skills to deliver on these focus areas?

- Do we have enough of these skills currently within our business?
  - If yes, are we well positioned to retain them? Are the people engaged and motivated?
  - If no, what is the best way to solve the gap? Should we build the talent internally or get the talent externally?
- Will we need these skills for the short term or for the long term?
- How available are these skills in the talent marketplace?

Moving to action: what you can do next

It is not enough to just have key skills and competencies identified. You must do something with them. You need to make them part of your organization's DNA. (Remember that bit about execution?) These competencies should be embedded in various HR processes and programmes. Think about your employee lifecycle – recruiting to exit – and where you can embed the competencies. Below are areas in the employee lifecycle to assess today:

Attraction and recruiting: When you post a new position, how are the key competencies required for the position outlined in the job description? Are they clear? When the recruiter interviews candidates, how do they check for these key skills? Be sure that the skills and competencies your organization values are clearly listed and described so candidates know what is required of them. Remember this is a marketing activity. Leverage your employer brand (we will talk more about this shortly) and specific language to attract the talent that you really want. Also, make it easy for those who are not a fit to self-select and not apply.

Onboarding: As part of the onboarding process, do managers sit down with their employees and discuss expectations based on the skills and competencies required for the job? Onboarding is also a good place to talk about the core values and how they tie in with the required skills and competencies. Beyond talking about them, how are they demonstrated when one comes on board? Do leaders show up? What is the experience like from a new employee perspective? Set the expectation through actions and behaviours.

Development and retention: At times of promotion, does the HR team and/or manager assess readiness for promotion based on the key competencies? Are there developmental opportunities, whether internal or external, that employees can attend to develop the skills necessary to achieve a promotion? This is where companies should be rigorous. Do not promote due to convenience or tenure. Set everyone up for success by developing the behaviours and skills to be successful at the next level.

Separation: If separation is due to a lack of required skills, is that readily documented? We also believe that if someone leaves as part of a career progression (maybe your organization isn't able to offer a promotion or more money based on your circumstances), they should leave with more skills and competencies than when they arrived. While ideally you would want to hold onto these people, sometimes it is simply not possible.

Lessons from the real world

What are the top two skills you think organizations will require in the future?

> Flexibility and digital proficiency are key skills for all workers as we look to the future. You can learn the specifics of an industry or the internal processes of a business, but you must be able to quickly shift and adapt as the needs of the business evolve. Also, in this post-COVID-19 world, place and space have shifted to the virtual realm. Training, collaboration, and service delivery are all occurring online and to succeed you must have not only basic digital literacy but a proficiency with a wide variety of tools being used to carry out every aspect of work. This includes an understanding of social media and web-based tools, business analytic and visualization tools, as well as collaboration and communication tools.

Brooke Valle, Chief Strategy and Innovation Officer at San Diego Workforce Partnership

Personally, I have always felt that you hire for work ethic and adaptability. When you have a hard-working team of people who are committed to your mission and values, you can teach them the skills and tools that they need to be successful at your company. If they are adaptable and have an innate sense of responsibility that comes from a strong work ethic, you can more effectively manage your business as it expands and/or contracts over time. You can then align your people, process, and technology to scale most effectively. This allows your team members to feel like they are being challenged, recognized, and rewarded. And it allows the business to hire for fit, rather than always looking for a 'unicorn' on paper.

Victoria Campbell, Vice President of People at The Honor Foundation

First, to be successful, organizations of all types must adapt to a constantly and more rapidly evolving competitive market, economic, labour and social dynamics that inevitably affect them. They can only do so if they are agile in how they organize people and work, plan and set goals, make decisions, and drive execution. This will require an entirely new way of thinking and approach to the way we work. Second, organizations will win if they can quickly connect the two greatest forces at work, human beings and information, with speed in ways that help them understand what their customers and employees truly need, synthesize those insights, and translate them to action faster than others.

Charlie Piscitello, Chief People Officer at Acutus Medical, Inc

What are two trends that you see with regards to talent in the future?

People will utilize technology to better understand how others feel (ie, happy, sad, anger, disgust, etc). People think they can accurately read body language. Technology can do it better... and will keep getting better. As our lives move online even more, this presents huge benefits to recruiting, training, coaching, sales, and many more areas. Referrals become even more critical. It has been said for years. It is more vital now. With fewer networking events, the challenges of meeting and getting to know people online, high unemployment, etc, every employee should become a recruiter. Teams will get better. Companies will become stronger.

Joel Stern, Senior Talent Acquisition Business Partner, Cue Health

It is easy to keep things transactional and impersonal through the use of technology. Technology has provided so much more autonomy and allows people to work remotely, but it will not substitute personal interactions. As we communicate more via email, text, and Instant Messaging, I am watching how leaders are finding it easier to not have difficult conversations with their teams and peers. Our ability to lean into difficult conversations face to face is diminishing and I believe that is impacting employee engagement and a company's results.

Tacy Riehm, Founder, Leadership Consultant, Speaker and Executive Coach at Vos Consulting, LLC

How does the COVID-19 pandemic change your prioritization of the skills needed for the future?

The skills needed to survive COVID and beyond, I believe, remain the same. They just become more important. Flexible and adaptable. Creative and innovative. Continuous learner. Relationship builder. This is only a partial list but a good start. Closely related, I believe, are processes that need to change. And this applies to people and companies. Embrace remote working. Utilize technology more. Ship fast and iterate even faster… nothing should wait to be 'perfect'.

Joel Stern, Senior Talent Acquisition Business Partner, Cue Health

Companies need to take a hard look at the technical and soft skills of their mid-level and mid-senior managers, and at their processes and systems. First and foremost, are your leaders effective communicators and are they able to truly lead by influence? Or are they just managing by metrics? Do they understand the strengths of their team members and the individual goals and interests that each person has and brings to the table? And are they leveraging them effectively? Making sure that our leaders have the skills to do this is a priority as our world is changing. This situation (COVID-19) has been a hard reset for us all in many ways. As companies grow, there is only ever so much money in the budget every year: for promotions, raises, adds to staff, technical improvements, etc... choices are made every year. As companies had to make the shift to remote environments, there were quite a few who did it exceptionally well. Those were the companies who had consistent, ongoing investment in leadership training, innovation, technology, and process training. As we look at the model for the future, I would say that continuing to anticipate these types of disruptions is prudent. Having leaders who have the leadership skills to be nimble and solve problems that have not been encountered before, and the humility to hire people who may be more technically skilled than they are is critical. Leadership means creating an environment where the team has the freedom to effectively perform their roles, within guidelines, to support the needs of the business. Leaders need to have the skills to know when to 'manage' and when to 'support'. They need to have an understanding of the strengths of the individuals on their team, and HOW to best leverage those strengths. And they need to be WILLING to leverage them.

Victoria Campbell, Vice President of People at The Honor Foundation

Final thoughts

Core competencies help ensure the skills, knowledge, and behaviours that employees need to possess are relevant and important to your organization. These core competencies help achieve business results and allow organizations to be successful in both the short and long term. Leadership competencies help create a strong image of what leadership looks like in your organization and the skills necessary to succeed as a leader. Core competencies can change over time depending on the stage of your company or a shift in priorities. However, when establishing your core competencies, consider any changes in the way work is done and be forward looking so you remain at the forefront of change.

Before we move on, take a few minutes to write down two to three key takeaways from this chapter with regards to your organization's core competencies. If you do not currently have any, consider how you will establish them. With this list in mind, next to each takeaway write down one action item that you will commit to doing to ensure your organization has core competencies that are infused in all aspects of your culture and programmes.

What are you committing to do?

Endnotes

1 Price, D (2020) I'm a tech CEO. Here's why I'm not taking a salary during Covid-19, *Fast Company*, 28 May, https://www.fastcompany.com/90510100/im-a-tech-ceo-heres-why-im-not-taking-a-salary-during-covid-19 (archived at https://perma.cc/3JGH-68BC)

2 Boerma, M *et al* (2017) Point/counterpoint: Are leaders born or made? *American Journal of Pharmaceutical Education*, https://www.ncbi.nlm.nih.gov/pmc/articles/PMC5423074/ (archived at https://perma.cc/XVM8-SRQN)

06

Attracting and retaining the right talent

To build a strong organizational culture, ensure that you embody transparency and empathy in clearly defining and articulating the organizational vision, mission, values and expected behaviours, while engaging employees to actively participate in defining what is important and why. Be sensitive to cross-cultural orientations and the variables that make up the different cultures of employees and their approaches to environment, time, action, communication, space, structure, etc that comprise your organization.

KATHY NAYLOR, GLOBAL HUMAN CAPITAL AND BUSINESS TRANSFORMATION ADVISER AND EXECUTIVE COACH AT CHANGE AND LEADERSHIP SOLUTIONS

By this point, you should be familiar with the type of culture your organization currently has and the culture you want to create. You should also have a plan to identify and define, or revisit, your organization's core values. Plus, you know the important skills that are needed to keep propelling your organization forward. Now it is time to attract the right talent with the skills you are looking for, and with your culture and core values in mind.

We are all familiar with the term 'war on talent'. But, do we really know what this even means and why it matters to our organization? The war on talent refers to how challenging it is to attract and retain the right type of talent. Organizations are not just looking for talent. They are looking for the best talent for their organization. They are looking for talent that can add value and add to their culture. Note that this applies for full-time hires, as well as resources you bring in to augment your team. As companies lean into the unbounded or elastic workforce, considering how you attract the right people matters.

Over the past 15 years, we have seen multiple examples where unemployment was soaring, and many people were challenged to find work. Even during those times, there were still certain types of skills along with types of employees that were in high demand. The competition for talent did not decrease across the board. Organizations were still hiring and looking for key talent to fill roles. That is true today, so therefore thinking about how to make your culture a competitive advantage is always a worthwhile thing to do.

You may be thinking, 'Talent is talent. It only matters for certain positions', but you'd be wrong. In fact, numerous studies have found that top, high-performing talent is exponentially more productive than average talent. According to a McKinsey & Company survey, high performers are anywhere from 50 to 800 per cent more productive than average performers when completing tasks that range from low complexity to very high complexity.[1] Think about these numbers in relation to your organization. If you replaced even 20 per cent of your average talent with top talent on a critical project, you would be able to complete your project sooner, resulting in getting a product or service to market faster, resulting in more profits sooner. The alternative is to let the top talent go to your competitor, who will get to market faster than you. We know which option we would choose.

In addition to an increase in productivity, hiring and retaining the right talent leads to an increase in employee engagement and motivation, which we will cover in the next chapter. First, you need to attract the top talent!

Why should someone work for your organization?

Take a few minutes and write down three reasons someone should work for your organization (and stay there once they are hired).

Common answers we hear to this question include: 'We're fun!' 'We're smart!' 'We pay well!' 'We're in a great location!' How many of your reasons included something along the same lines as the answers given above?

Why someone should work for your organization can be a hard question to answer if you have not spent time cultivating a strong culture that attracts the right talent. Dig deeper than ping pong tables and free snacks (which is not the reason people want to work for you, trust us). The truth is… none of these reasons really answer the question of why someone should work for you.

Think about your own personal reasons for a moment. Why do you work for your organization? The reasons are probably deeper than the ones we mentioned above. They are also a lot more personal. They are probably the reasons that others may want to work for your organization as well. But does your recruitment process convey those reasons effectively or are they hidden behind the *beer keg in the breakroom* and *every other Friday off* pitches?

How exactly do you convey these meaningful reasons, so that you are attracting the right talent? You create a strong Employee Value Proposition (or EVP). The EVP is critical to attracting and attaining the right talent. Your EVP is not about how much you pay or the free stuff that you offer. It is about who you are and what it is like to work for your organization. It is more about the personal reasons you gave for why you work at your organization. And a strong EVP accurately conveys your culture, the essence of who you are. Think of your EVP like a deal or agreement – in exchange for the skills, talents, and experiences that you will bring to the organization, this is what you will get in return. The EVP is how you distinguish your organization from your competition.

Another way to think of the EVP is like a Customer Value Proposition. The Customer Value Proposition is a mental/psychological framework for people to make decisions. Something in the value proposition connected (or did not connect) with them. As a consumer, why do you buy one brand of laundry detergent over another? What attracts you to a specific TV brand? Why do you use the bank you do versus its competitor? The brands you choose to buy and the companies you choose to do business with have a very specific customer in mind.

They have a small window to convey to you what problem they solve better than their competitor and why you should choose them.

The EVP works the same way. The EVP is not about attracting *all* candidates. It is about attracting the *right* candidates for your organization. You do that as an organization by being authentically clear as to who you are and how working for your organization is *better* than working for anyone else's organization. Just like when you acknowledge that customers have choice in who they do business with, talent has choices today too. In fact, top talent has even more.

THERE ARE MANY ORGANIZATIONS WITH AMAZING EVPS

Take Canva for one. Canva, based in Australia, offers a graphic design tool. While the company offers many perks, like in-house chefs and gym memberships, they also clearly outline how each employee directly impacts their mission. On the 'Why Canva?' page of their website, they clearly provide the '5 reasons why you should join Canva'. They touch on individual impact, the many design projects employees work on (34 million per month to be exact), the opportunity for personal and professional development, sustainability initiatives, and their people. Each area is succinctly described in one or two sentences. Canva takes it one step further, even listing their values directly on their website. And before going into the open positions, they break it down with a section on Life at Canva. The EVP is simple, clear, and speaks to the type of employee they want to attract.

Another company with a strong EVP on a global scale is Unilever, a British-Dutch consumer goods company behind some of the most popular and widely used brands in the world. Again, directly from the Careers page on their website, Unilever has a section titled 'Why Work for Unilever'. Their EVP is broken out into four pillars: Purpose Power, Be the Catalyst, Brilliantly Different Together, and Go Beyond. Each section goes into further detail about the pillar and features actual Unilever employees. At the top of the page, their EVP reads: 'Unilever is the place where you can bring your purpose to life through the work that you do, creating a better business and a better world. You will work with brands that are loved and improve the lives of our consumers and the communities around us.' Two impactful and powerful sentences sending a direct message to candidates as to who Unilever is and how employees contribute to the mission.

FIGURE 6.1 Creating an EVP

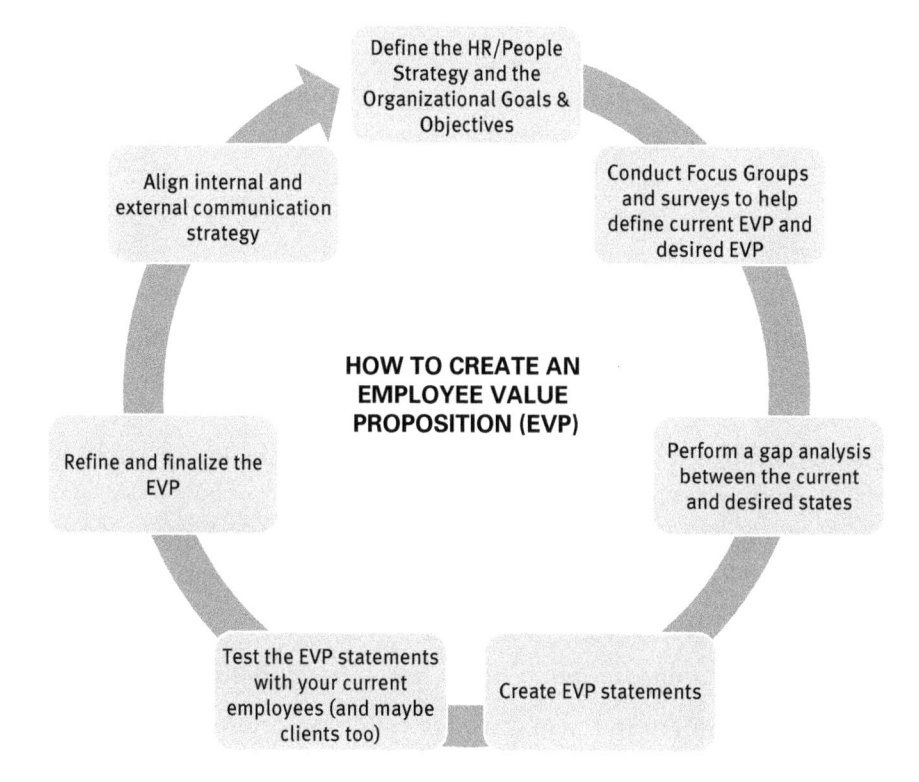

HOW TO CREATE AN EMPLOYEE VALUE PROPOSITION (EVP)

- Define the HR/People Strategy and the Organizational Goals & Objectives
- Conduct Focus Groups and surveys to help define current EVP and desired EVP
- Perform a gap analysis between the current and desired states
- Create EVP statements
- Test the EVP statements with your current employees (and maybe clients too)
- Refine and finalize the EVP
- Align internal and external communication strategy

Much like identifying and defining your organizational core values, creating an EVP is a process and should not be rushed. Figure 6.1 outlines the steps for creating an EVP. These steps generally apply if this is the first time you are creating a formal EVP. However, some of these steps are still relevant if you are revisiting your EVP to see if it is still accurate.

Prior to starting on the journey of creating an EVP, make sure the right people are in the room. This team could be the same group as your core values team. For this group, having a marketing lens is going to be important, so be sure there is someone from your marketing department on the team. This lens is important so you can align your employee brand with your customer/client brand. It is not unusual to only have one or two members of the executive team represented on the team rather than all executives. However, as an executive team be sure that you are all aligned so whatever is being communicated in the EVP team meetings by the executive team member is representative of the intentions of the whole executive team.

In order to gain this alignment, it may be beneficial for your head of HR or head of people to lead a discussion around who you want to be in terms of talent, what features and characteristics you would like that set you apart from the competition, etc. This alignment is going to be critical at time of rollout as well.

Once the team is assembled, but before you create the EVP, you first need to know your HR/people strategy, along with the organizational goals and objectives. These are important because you need to attract top talent that can help you achieve your business objectives. These objectives also help define the right type of talent you need and the skills they need to possess.

Then, you must understand what your EVP is today (even if it is not a formally defined EVP, you do have one). Think about the EVP in four different buckets:

- *Rewards*: Compensation, benefits, time off, flexibility.
- *Culture*: Leaders and managers, colleagues, support system, social responsibility.
- *Work environment/organization*: Autonomy, understanding of organization's strategy and goals, challenges.
- *Career/opportunity*: Stability, development and growth, feedback.

To help you better understand your EVP today, conduct focus groups. Many of the questions you asked during the core values focus groups would also be valuable to ask your EVP group. They are designed to give you an idea of the current environment, what is valued and why people work at your organization. A few other questions to ask include:

- What work are you most proud of and why?
- If you were considering accepting a job from another organization and pay was equal, what would make you want to stay with us?
- How satisfied are you with your ability to learn, grow and develop here?

- How satisfied are you with the recognition you have received for the work you have done?
- Do you feel supported by your management team to have a life outside of the organization and to pursue personal interests?
- What would make us an exciting engagement for a high-demand, highly skilled contractor?

Some of the questions are open ended, while others are on the Likert scale (strongly agree all the way to strongly disagree) and are designed to get at the heart of each of the EVP buckets we previously mentioned. Make sure that when you are asking questions, they are focused on these buckets. You can always ask a question around, 'Is there anything we haven't talked about today or that doesn't fit into these buckets that you think is important to our culture and who we are?' Do not forget to also ask your EVP team the same questions. Again, you picked this group for a reason. Their answers and input to the questions are going to be important. In addition, don't forget to talk to your HR team. The Talent Acquisition team is going to be a good source of information on why candidates are choosing your company over others or, vice versa, why you may be losing candidates to competitors. As an aside, be sure to have a member of the Talent Acquisition team on your EVP team. Your HR Business Partners are also a good source of information around some common issues they are seeing in their client groups and which ones are related to the four EVP buckets. The Business Partners will also have insights into terminations and why talent is leaving your organization. Tap into all of your resources, both internal and external, to get a comprehensive picture. You do not want to be continuously adjusting your EVP.

Once you have the data, look at common themes and trends. Then, conduct a gap analysis between the current state and the desired future state. To do this, compare where you are today based on what employees have said and where you would like to be. This is the 'gap'. You may fall short of the desired state, and that is okay. The important part is to be realistic. An EVP is not meant to be aspirational, but inspirational. This gap is also important to discuss with your executive team. If you have the data, use it. Use the gap analysis to talk about areas that require immediate attention and areas that may be okay for now but will need to be addressed in the future. This data is a good blueprint of employee sentiment and helps inform future objectives and goals related to culture and talent.

After conducting the gap analysis, use your data to create an EVP. This can be a few sentences or broken down into those four areas previously mentioned. Think back to Canva and Unilever. They provided multiple statements based on separate yet connected themes or areas that employees find most important. On the other hand, HubSpot, a US-based business-to-business (b2b) software development organization, has narrowed it down to one sentence on their website: 'Our goal is to help you be the best "you" that you can be, both inside and outside of work.' Whichever option you choose, whether multiple sentences or just one, be sure it rings true to your culture today.

This next step is one of the most crucial. After you create the EVP, test it! Test the statements throughout the organization, either by department/division or in focus groups. This method serves two purposes: by testing an EVP internally, you get more information about your brand *and* you connect with your employees and make them part of the solution. They feel like they have a say in the type of talent that should work for your organization and the type of culture that is being created. You may also find some unintended consequences of the statements that were created. For example, they may be realistic to 90 per cent of the positions in your organization, but there could be a department where they do not apply. An example of this can be customer service departments. Many of the benefits or perks recognized by others in the organization may not be viewed the same by employees who are tethered to their desks due to being on the phone all day. Once you have thoroughly tested the statements and refined them as necessary, then you can move to launching and rolling them out.

After testing the EVP statements internally and before launch, be sure to have a strong communication plan. You will want to be sure your HR programmes and policies are aligned to this EVP, so you are doing and acting in accordance with your EVP. You will also want to communicate the new EVP broadly to all of your employees. Make sure your EVP is also represented accurately in your client and customer-facing communications. You want the messaging and branding to be cohesive and consistent. How will you flaunt your EVP? Will you create a video? Clearly articulate it on your website? Or have executives mention different benefits and values in their communications? Our suggestion would be that you do all of the above. You have invested time and money into creating a strong EVP. You should be proud of that accomplishment and it should be represented in everything you do. Remember, culture is a brand and your EVP is how you articulate that brand.

We have seen the rollout and launch of an EVP done really well as a cross-functional project. This does not clearly belong to HR or marketing; rather, when the teams work together, it can create a powerful opportunity. In one case, our client was going through a full re-branding exercise and used this as an opportunity to also establish their EVP. This ensured that both messages were aligned in tone and positioning, while also enrolling the internal stakeholders and employees in both.

By ensuring all necessary and relevant stakeholders are involved, the EVP gets operationalized through organizational processes and forms. HR can update things like policies, job posting templates, hiring documents, and internal communications while marketing can ensure the website, client surveys, and client marketing efforts are updated to reflect and support the established EVP. Whether creating an EVP for the first time or updating one that currently exists, the success or failure lies within the change management: as you can see, the EVP has a lot of moving pieces. In Chapter 10, we cover some change management principles that you can use to ensure your EVP is a success.

While not an official step, it is essential to check in with your EVP. At the executive level, you can turn this into an item to discuss every quarter or every six months to ensure that the EVP is still accurate and that all internal and external programmes and communications align with it. Do not forget to check in with your employees through pulse surveys and engagement surveys. While you do not want to rewrite your EVP frequently, you should at least check in and make small adjustments as necessary to ensure it stays relevant and true to your organizational identity.

> **CULTURE QUOTE**
>
> Culture is like a garden. It has to constantly be tended and cultivated. My best advice to a leader is to ensure that they are hiring the right people and then letting them do the job that they were hired to do. Don't be afraid of change (in people, process, or technology). Allow the 'what if' and possibility conversations to occur. It helps build camaraderie and stimulate creative ideas to solve problems. As a company, get clear on why you exist and what your purpose is. There has to be a reason that you make your product and sell it, and you need to be able to explain what it is so that your team can connect to it. Look for employees who have a similar reason for wanting to be there. They will connect with the mission in a way that makes them want to add value far beyond their job description. Let them do that. Listen to people. The best ideas come from people who have the freedom to express them... not just the most senior leaders or the person with the degree from the best college. And lastly, if you ask for an opinion or input, make sure you acknowledge receiving it. Nothing erodes trust faster than people feeling like they haven't been heard or acknowledged. This doesn't mean you act on every idea. Just acknowledge the idea or suggestion... or don't ask for input.
>
> *Victoria Campbell, Vice President of People, The Honor Foundation*

Using the EVP to attract the right talent

Once you have established your EVP and have your career page and all collateral aligned, you may notice a change in the candidate pool. While this clarity can narrow your candidate pool sometimes, you can be left with some amazing high performers who are engaged with the mission, purpose, and culture. On the other hand, if your EVP is really strong and your organization is bigger, you may have just opened up your candidate pool to hundreds more applicants all vying to work for you. Your EVP works like a magnet. While you will attract a lot of different types of talent, you will want to be sure you focus on the talent that is right for the particular position you are recruiting for.

One way to do this is to tailor your messaging to specific types of roles. For example, in some positions, highlighting the organization as a whole may be beneficial, while in others, focusing on the work itself may be the key. You are not creating different EVPs. You are highlighting portions of your EVP based on the role you are hiring for. In much the same fashion, all employees value different things based on the stage of life they are in. If you have a candidate who is great for your role and you know they have a family, mention some of the family-friendly benefits you have, such as 'Bring your child to work day' or additional time off for new parents. On the other hand, if you know a candidate values travelling and experiencing the world, make mention of your generous paid time off plan. These are all benefits that are part of your EVP, but you are pulling certain levers and individualizing what is meaningful to the candidate. There will be more on the individualization of rewards in Chapter 8.

Opting out is okay

The goal of the EVP is to help you attract the right type of talent for your organization. Sometimes, candidates can seem like they are a good fit on the surface, but once you start the interview process and start diving into their experience, it can quickly become evident that they may not possess the values or the skills you are looking for. At this stage, it is early enough, and you have not hired anyone, so no harm no foul. Just be sure to treat all candidates with respect. Remember, every interaction affects your brand as well as your organization's brand.

But what happens if you hire someone who turns out *not* to be a good fit, especially early on in their employment? Are you stuck with them? Perhaps the first company to make an 'opt out' bonus popular was Zappos, an online shoe and clothing retailer based in Las Vegas,

Nevada. Upon hire, all new employees enter a four-week immersive onboarding experience where they learn about the organization's strategy, culture, and customers while receiving their regular salary.

This immersive onboarding is required of all new hires, from a customer service representative to the head of HR. At the end of the four-week experience, employees are given The Offer. The Offer goes something like this: 'If you quit today, we'll pay you $1,000. No questions asked.'[2] Yep, Zappos will pay employees to quit! It is not as far-fetched as it sounds. If an employee takes the $1,000, they are not the type of employee Zappos wants as part of the organization and culture. They want people who are aligned with their mission, level of customer service, and strategy. In 2015, we visited Zappos as part of their Zappos Insights for Executives. Throughout our two days onsite, we can attest to the fact that, while The Offer is a bit unorthodox, the employees who remained were engaged, truly excited for the work they do, and aligned to the organization's philosophy and vision.

Once Zappos was purchased by Amazon in 2009, Amazon continued The Offer in a different way. This time, the programme was called Pay to Quit.[3] This was less about new employees and more about *all* employees. Once a year, Amazon offers employees up to $5,000 to quit. The longer the tenure, the higher the number. Amazon does not want employees who do not want to be there. These employees hurt the culture, hurt productivity, and mar their reputation. With that said, Amazon hopes people do not take the offer. In fact, the email that CEO Jeff Bezos, sends is titled 'Please don't take this offer'.

Even if you do not want to pay employees to quit, it is still important to set an 'opt out' strategy. This is really where it is vital to be super clear around expectations and performance metrics. While we will cover this in more detail in the next chapter as it relates to engaging and motivating employees, setting expectations early with new hires is important. By doing so, managers also have clear, objective criteria to measure performance, and if there is an issue, it can be easier as an organization to start the 'opt out' process early.

A values fit is more important than a culture fit

People often struggle to describe the difference between culture and values and, more often than not, people assume they are one and the same. This actually isn't true. For us, values guide decision making. In other words, they are how we make decisions. Culture is the collective of the interactions, processes, and business practices within each organization. Culture can change and morph with the business. Values generally stay the same. If an organization veers away from their values, the culture is affected.

The term *culture fit* has been used for years in the hiring process. Some people swear by it as a reason to hire while others say it is discriminatory. In our experience, we have often seen it as a 'reason' not to hire someone. We use the word 'reason' loosely here, because to base a hiring decision on a feeling or a bias, which culture fit implies, is not okay. In fact, within the term *culture fit*, there is an implicit bias. We tend to hire people whom we like. People we have something in common with. Maybe our kids go to the same school, maybe we went to the same university, maybe we have similar work ethics.

We jump to the conclusion that because we have these one or two things in common, they are just like us. And because they are just like us, they will fit into the culture we have created. While this can be true, it is not always the case. When we hire based on culture fit, we tend to hire people who think like us. Act like us. Maybe even look like us. This greatly affects our ability for diverse viewpoints and experiences. Part of the issue is we have become accustomed to reviewing résumés/CVs and talking to candidates to determine whether someone would be a good fit or not. This process can cause biases as well. For example, a résumé with an Ivy League school listed can be viewed more favourably than a résumé with a non-Ivy League school. Our bias could lead us to believe that the candidate with the Ivy League alma mater is more qualified because of their education. To eliminate this type of bias and to focus on skills, some organizations are using software programs to redact name, university and even pictures.

Values-based hiring, on the other hand, produces diversity in thought, experiences, decisions, and solutions with the underlying foundation always being based in the values of the organization. This also allows for disagreements, which can often lead to better outcomes and strategies because the disagreements are handled respectfully.

How do you find out if your organization's values align with the candidate's? During interviews, we often hear culture questions asked, such as, 'Are you willing to work long hours, including the weekends, if necessary?' or 'Do you prefer to work in an office or remotely?'

But what about the values questions?

One of our clients, a consumer finance company, puts their values at the forefront of hiring. In partnership, we created a Culture Committee with representatives from all levels and departments throughout the organization. Selection for this committee was based on a nomination process followed by interviews to ensure the members practise the values in their everyday work and through their actions.

One of the key responsibilities of this committee is to conduct values interviews with all candidates who are interviewing for a position at the organization. Where possible, the committee member chosen to conduct the interview is from a different department than the one the candidate is applying to. And often, the committee member may not even know the position that is being interviewed for.

The values interview is not about the candidate's skills, experience, or abilities to fulfil the requirements of the job. The values interview is about gaining a better understanding of the candidate's actions, or the how. It is about how they complete tasks, handle stress, manage through challenges and crises. The questions are based on the candidate's own experiences, known as behavioural-based interviewing.

For example:

- *Describe a time where you had to go above and beyond to keep your commitment to a co-worker or client.*
- *What steps do you personally take to build trust with a manager and co-workers?*

- *Tell me about a time when you had to deliver on a commitment that was difficult for you.*

The interviewer is not concerned with the context or the details of these scenarios. They are listening for how the candidate behaved and acted, ie demonstrating trust, integrity, respect, etc.

Just because you may have hired employees who are aligned with your values, what about the employees you hired from before this practice? Or what about the employees who stray from the values? Values are even more important when it comes to retention, so how do you figure out if you have a values misalignment?

Tell us if any of these sound familiar:

- *It's just how he is…*
- *But she's excellent with clients and her sales are the highest on the team.*
- *He is one of the best technically. So what if people skills aren't his strength?*

If you are hearing this kind of feedback, it is an indicator that you may have a values misalignment. If there is a values misalignment, taking action and not letting the behaviour turn into 'that's just how so and so is' is key. Building values into performance management is already critical, not just from an alignment perspective, but from an engagement and motivation perspective too.

If you are excusing bad behaviour for any reason, people see it. The message you send is that you are not serious about your values and that you prioritize other things first, like getting that sale or advancing technology faster. It says that you value the 'what' more than the 'how'.

It is like creating an excuse for people to act outside your values. At that point, you've completely undermined values within your organization. As tough as it is, we recommend taking a zero-tolerance approach to upholding your values. That doesn't mean you have to fire someone for a first infraction, but it does mean that you address them as they come up, don't let infractions go unacknowledged, and view it as your role to be the model about what is expected in a consistent manner across the organization.

Recruiting leaders

We would be remiss if we did not talk for a few minutes about hiring leaders and other executives into your organization. When it comes to hiring executives, it is natural for us to want the most technically strong and 'good at their job' individual. In fact, we often try to attract executives from competitors or other organizations in the same or similar industry as us. The problem occurs when their values don't necessarily align with those of your organization. As CEO, it is your job to call this out and not become enamoured by their list of accomplishments. As HR leader, it is your job to keep the culture and values lens on all hires, especially executive hires. As we've said numerous times before, people are watching the behaviours of the executive team way more than you think. If you are trying to create a certain type of culture, ask yourself whether the executive you are considering is a values fit and culture add or whether they will create a toxic culture.

Common pitfalls

There is a 1989 movie, *Field of Dreams*, about a farmer who hears a voice that eventually leads him to build a baseball diamond where the ghosts of legendary baseball players come to play. The mysterious voice says one thing: 'If you build it, they will come'. Much like organizational structure, think of culture and your EVP in the same way. If you build a strong culture around core values and are able to clearly articulate that culture through the EVP, then good talent will follow. However, there are definitely some pitfalls to look out for when trying to attract the right talent. Below are a few of the most common:

Active hiring will attract the 'qualified and not looking' crowd. You post the job, your EVP is out there and now you wait. Anyone who wants to work for you will definitely apply. Right? Wrong. If you want qualified talent, you have to go out and get it. That means approaching the candidates who are qualified (this is called sourcing), talking to them about your organization and the role. While many people are not actively looking for a new position if they are happy where they are, most are open to considering what else is out there if the price and culture are right. Do not assume passive candidates will come to you. Go after them!

Not leveraging internal talent for new positions. Within your organization, what percentage of new positions were filled through internal promotions? If you said not too many, you are not alone. As soon as a new position is created, most organizations post it on external sites to begin advertising. But, by posting it internally first, you may be surprised at who could be interested and qualified for the position. Plus, you have already hired them once, they know your values and culture and, most importantly, they know how your organization functions. While not every internal candidate is qualified, we would suggest having an internal posting policy in which you post your positions internally for at least one or two weeks first, before posting them externally. Consider what you do internally to make people aware of these opportunities. One idea is to send a weekly digest of open roles or newly posted roles as an email update. This can work both to send the message that there are internal opportunities and that people don't need to look externally for new roles, and will spark people to think of great referrals for these jobs if they know someone great.

One-size-fits-all approach. What attracted you to the organization is going to be different to what attracted one of your employees to the organization. It is important to keep this in mind when hiring. For example, if you are looking to hire for entry-level positions, perhaps recent college graduates are a target candidate pool for you. In this case, highlight your fun work environment and career advancement opportunities as a way to attract them. We tend to see this pitfall with smaller or start-up organizations where employees wear multiple hats and there may not be a dedicated HR leader. In this case, whoever is responsible for hiring should spend a little time on customizing their approach based on the type of candidate they are trying to hire. This will go a long way as the culture and organization mature.

Boring job descriptions. Many leaders are in such a hurry these days that they do not spend time really thinking about the job description for the role they need to fill. Instead, they are too focused on hurrying to get the job posted to quickly hire a candidate to fill a gap. When this happens, we simply find the old job description, dust it off and repost it. The language is most likely stale and routine: 'Must have 10+ years of experience', or 'strong communication skills required'. Hardly do we think about the effect the language we use in our job descriptions has on attracting the top talent we are looking for. But language matters. Use language that will attract the type of candidate you are looking for. For example, in accounting you need a keen attention to detail. Instead of writing that exact phrase, consider the type of person who would fit well with your values and culture and who is qualified for the job. Maybe a phrase such as, 'Your attention to detail is so high that anything less drives you crazy'. Your job descriptions are a great way for you to showcase your culture and values, yet most organizations do not take advantage of them.

A fixed process defined by forms and red tape. 'We have three rounds of interviews; you'll be onsite for eight hours.' Depending on the type of culture you are trying to create and what your EVP states, eight hours of interviews may be off-putting to your ideal candidate. While the process length should be reasonable, it should also speak to the type of culture and organization you are. To us, eight hours of interviews would signify that there is a lot of bureaucratic red tape to make decisions and that the culture is perhaps a bit formal. In addition, when candidates apply for positions, are they forced to create an account, upload a résumé/CV, and then provide their home address, answer questions about their experience, etc? The process can already seem lengthy for passive candidates, so they then may opt out altogether. When posting positions, think about the minimum amount of information you need in order to determine if the candidate is interesting enough to pursue. In terms of the interview process, keep your culture in mind and ask yourself, 'What does our process say about the type of organization we truly are?'

Questions to ask

As previously mentioned, your EVP should paint a clear picture of what it is like to work for your organization today. The box below provides questions for you as the CEO or HR leader to ask yourself and members of your executive team to determine whether your EVP is having the desired impact.

QUESTIONS TO ASK – ASSESSING YOUR EVP: EXECUTIVE VIEW

- How different is our EVP from the organizations with whom we compete for talent?
- What makes us unique?
- What is the candidate persona (ideal candidate) we want to attract and retain based on where the business is today? (And where we see it going in the next five years?)
- Does our EVP match the attributes that persona is looking for in an organization?
- What does Glassdoor (and other social sites) say about what it is like to work here?
- Is what was important to us as an organization when we created the EVP still important to us today? Would our employees agree?

Moving to action: what you can do next

Below are some actionable steps you can take today to ensure you are attracting the right talent for your organization. Check in with these steps frequently to ensure your talent attraction and retention strategies clearly communicate your culture:

Look at leadership. If there is dysfunction at the top, regardless of how amazing your EVP is, you will not be able to retain, let alone attract, the top talent you need. Alignment at the leadership level is fundamental to ensuring your EVP is accurate. You can have the best EVP in the world, but if your leadership team is not effective, that EVP will not matter.

Revamp your interview questions. Ask questions that get to someone's motivations and personality. Earlier we mentioned the types of questions to ask to assess the candidate's core values. Another way to get to know someone is through hypothetical questions: If you had two weeks off every summer and were continuing to get paid during that time, what would you do? Questions such as this provide insights into a candidate's energy level, risk level, etc. They are also a nice way to get to know your candidate in a more holistic manner.

Get real. Write down what you think your organization's EVP is. Then ask other members of your team what *they* think your organization's EVP is. Compare the two. Are they similar or vastly different?

Get educated. As CEO, meet with your HR leader or HR team to determine if your organization has an EVP, but you may just not be aware of it. If you do have one, find out what it is and how it is embedded into your culture. Do not stop there. Ensure all members of your executive team are aware of your EVP. If you do not have an EVP, start the process mentioned earlier in this chapter.

Get creative. Think about your hiring process. Are there areas where you can improve? Perhaps incorporate values into the interview process? If you have something unique about your culture or values, the interview is a great time to talk about it. Give employees the option to opt out too. And do not take it personally. You want employees who are committed to you just as much as you are to them.

Lessons from the real world

In your experience, what is the number one key to attracting and retaining top talent?

> The number one key to attracting and retaining top talent is to reimagine what 'top talent' means. Not every person is right for every job in your company. Rather than view a select few employees as 'high potentials', view all employees as having potential – it just may be in a different area than first envisioned. To unlock the key of how to attract and retain talent, we need to effectively design a culture where all are

welcomed and embraced for who they are and what they add to the culture – not how they fit into the culture. We must be flexible and adapt our companies and how we work to our employees and potential employees – not the other way around.

Tracie Sponenberg, Chief People Officer of The Granite Group

I believe that providing a quality job, not because you have to but because you know it is the right thing to do, is one of the most important keys to attracting and retaining top talent in any field. For me, job quality is the combination of job necessities (things like pay and appropriate classification), job opportunities (growth and development) and job features (benefits, experiences, interesting opportunities). Job necessities create the conditions for fair work, job opportunities maximize individual and organizational potential, and job features respond to the individual needs of the worker.

Brooke Valle, Chief Strategy and Innovation Officer at San Diego Workforce Partnership

When should an organization create their EVP?

Yesterday! The EVP is critical, and must be linked to and reflect strategy, culture, and the talent management strategy. Employers that lack an EVP are missing the boat. It's job one for talent attraction. Research has shown that the employment brand is much more of an attractor than the parent brand, except for a few highly recognizable brands (Google, Facebook, Netflix, Disney, etc).

Roberto Blain, Principal at Cerulean Leadership and Adjunct Faculty at University of Southern California, Bovard College

An organization should create their EVP as soon as possible, as it is essential when trying to brand your company to potential employees. Your EVP will explain, in a few short sentences, what the experience of working for your company is like. That needs to be out in front of your potential audience sooner than later, or you will fall behind.

Tracie Sponenberg, Chief People Officer of The Granite Group

Final thoughts

EVPs can be the differentiator between an extraordinary culture and a culture that is just good. They serve as a way for you to tell your organization's story to the world to not only attract and retain top talent, but to improve your organization's brand and reputation in the marketplace. As CEO, it is important for you to be part of the EVP story. You are, after all, captain of the ship. As HR leader, do not put the EVP on the back burner. Make it the star of the show and ensure it stays relevant.

Before moving on, take a few minutes to write down two to three key takeaways from this chapter with regards to your organization's ability to attract and retain top talent. Think about aspects of the hiring process that may be working well and areas which could use some attention. Also think about your current retention strategies. Are they working for you? Now, looking at that list, next to each takeaway write down one action item that you will commit to doing to ensure your organization is an employer of choice.

What will you commit to?

Endnotes

1 Keller, S and Meaney, M (2017) Attracting and retaining the right talent, *McKinsey*, 24 November, https://www.mckinsey.com/business-functions/organization/our-insights/attracting-and-retaining-the-right-talent (archived at https://perma.cc/9TL8-DBPU)

2 Taylor, B (2008) Why Zappos pays new employees to quit–and you should too, *Harvard Business Review*, 19 May, https://hbr.org/2008/05/why-zappos-pays-new-employees (archived at https://perma.cc/WV66-GYYJ)

3 Semuels, A (2018) Why Amazon pays some of its workers to quit, *The Atlantic*, 14 February, https://www.theatlantic.com/business/archive/2018/02/amazon-offer-pay-quit/553202/#:~:text=And%20if%20they%20do%2C%20Amazon,unhappy%20employees%20to%20move%20on (archived at https://perma.cc/C5E3-FGNA)

07

Engagement and motivation

It's imperative to have frequent, honest and transparent communication from the top down to the front line. Give the people the benefit of the doubt that they can handle bad news like adults. If they don't believe they are hearing the absolute truth from their leaders, trust is eroded, and they will make up stories that are usually much worse than the actual truth.

LAURIE MILLER, EXECUTIVE VICE PRESIDENT,
HUMAN RESOURCES, MARKETING AND COMMUNICATIONS
AT ALLIANCE HEALTHCARE SERVICES

Employee engagement has become a buzzword. We all want to inspire and motivate our employees and teams. We want to encourage people to bring their discretionary effort to their work. Having a culture with high trust is critical to both engaging and motivating employees. How do you create a high-trust culture? It is deeper than just trusting your employees. You have to set clear expectations and then empower them to do their jobs. You have to make sure they have the tools, training, and resources to be successful. You have to be sure they have an avenue to make appropriate requests in the event they do not have the right resources. Then, you must provide those resources so they can effectively do their jobs.

You also must understand the three key questions employees ask of their managers:

1 Do you care about me?

2 Can I trust you?

3 Do you have my back?

Managers should be working to reinforce these questions in a consistent manner for all of their direct reports. People watch not only how you treat them, but how you treat others. So, if there are managers who demonstrate these three things in an inconsistent fashion, it will undermine trust and confidence across the board, even with those who they work hard to make feel valued and cared for.

Consistent accountability and direct feedback are also important for trust. In turn, trust builds loyalty. It is this loyalty that makes the high performers stay and continue taking care of the business. Trust and loyalty do not come from just having a connection to the work or the purpose of the organization. They come from the leader. Meaningful work will only take an employee so far. At some point, they want to know that their manager hears them and is there for them. This is where the accountability and feedback come into play. Unfortunately, we often see certain values hinder the trust.

In our line of work, we see cultures where 'niceness' results in people not being held accountable. This is actually not nice. It is not nice to all the other employees who are working hard to live the values and produce high levels of results. It is not nice because managers are not giving them the opportunity of direct feedback to improve. This can only be tolerated for so long before either manager or team frustration will cause a required action, which turns the situation into an emergency. It is hard to jump straight to firing someone if you have not taken the other mitigating steps, right? This lack of action results in your top-performing employees losing momentum and eventually leaving.

According to a 2019 Work Institute Retention Report, the top three reasons employees left an organization in 2018 were a lack of career development (22.2 per cent), work-life balance (12 per cent), and their manager's behaviour (11.4 per cent).[1] Often, organizations, and leaders in particular, think that the reason employees leave is due to money. They also believe the inverse of this – that the best way to engage and motivate employees is through money. In fact, in our careers, we have often seen leaders throw money at employees in an effort to get them to stay, and three months later, the employee leaves anyway. This is sadly pretty common, and we are sure you've seen this in your career as well. There is also an unintended consequence of this action: employees talk. They know when someone has received more money and they can view it as a way to buy back loyalty. This only further works to erode trust. It is deeper than just that one employee leaving; it's the trickle-down impact that eventually spreads across the culture.

While there are countless studies and reports like the one mentioned above, we are going to talk about two areas that, when done incorrectly, can derail your entire culture, turning once high-performing employees into unmotivated, disengaged culture killers: engagement surveys and the simple art of listening.

To do or not to do: engagement surveys?

Imagine your significant other is getting ready for a big business meeting and they ask you which shirt to wear: blue or red? You answer blue, feeling happy that they asked your opinion. They decide to wear the red one. Happiness has turned to frustration as you stand there wondering, 'Then why did you ask me?' That is what employees feel like when taking engagement surveys. What starts as optimism at being asked for an opinion fades to anger and resentment when nothing is done with their feedback.

How many of these statements sound familiar?

- We should ask employees what they think.
- We have not done a survey in a while. We should do one.
- It has been three months since our last survey. Let's check in with employees again.

As CEO, once you make these statements, you start a chain reaction where HR starts to prepare the survey, it is sent out, responses come in. Then what happens? Perhaps you say:

- I don't think this is how they really feel.
- We have shifted our focus and don't need those survey results anymore.
- It says x, what I think they mean is y.
- Interesting. I was wondering how they felt. Now I know. Let's move on.

Sadly, the fourth response above is one we hear when we are called in to help. Engagement surveys are not an exercise in curiosity. They are time-consuming and can be expensive to conduct, depending on how many employees you have and if you use an external vendor. The data is to inform meaningful action and improvement. You need to be willing to hear things that you may not be fully ready to face. Then, you must be prepared and committed to take action.

There is an underlying assumption that employee engagement surveys are designed to measure employee engagement. The truth is, they are designed to *improve* employee engagement. Why bother asking how people are doing if you have no intention of turning an 'okay' into a 'great'?

For example, when we meet with clients for the first time, they often tell us that they survey their employees annually, so they have a lot of good data. Some even do a six-month pulse check-in. Our very first question is always, 'What have you done with the data?'

We're not psychic, but 9 times out of 10 we already know the answer… nothing. They have not done anything with the data because priorities shifted, a new leader came in, or they did not know where to start.

Because. Because. Because. Each one of these excuses results in employees losing motivation and becoming disengaged. In fact, when we talk to the employees in these organizations, we often hear that they feel the surveys are a joke and that leadership does not really want to hear what they have to say. They do not take the surveys seriously.

Long story short, unless organizations have a plan in place on how to respond to the data from surveys, it is best not to ask employees their opinions. The feedback they provide is real. By asking for their feedback, there is a perception that the organization cares and will, therefore, listen to the feedback and take action appropriately. When this does not happen, employees become discouraged and the perception can be that the organization simply does not care. Remember, perception is reality.

Using surveys for good

However, asking your employees for their feedback and opinion is actually a great way to involve everyone in the future and direction of your organization and especially in shaping the culture. Employees want to feel part of the solution and they want to be heard. So, before embarking on an engagement survey, have a plan in place as to what you plan to do with the results and how you plan to communicate them.

This does not mean that you must take action on every single item that came up on the survey. Employees do not expect you to. But they do expect you to take action on the bigger items as well as the items that have shown up multiple times on each survey. Below are some questions you can ask yourself and the rest of your leadership team before embarking on the employee survey journey:

- *What are we trying to accomplish or learn through this survey?* Remember design thinking from Chapter 3? This is similar to that in that you need to start with the desired outcome in mind. This will allow you to stay focused and help you determine the best course of action and questions to accomplish your mission. As part of this question, you should also answer how you will measure what you are trying to learn or accomplish. Can it be measured in an engagement survey or are there other ways to measure it?
- *How long will the survey take our employees?* Ideally, surveys should take no more than 5–15 minutes depending on how many questions you are asking. If you do decide an engagement survey is the best way to learn about what you want to measure, then do not

make the actual survey too time consuming. Employees already have a lot of tasks and projects and the survey should not be viewed as something that will just take too much time to complete. Keep it simple!

- *Are we committed to making changes?* As we mentioned above, unless there is a strong commitment from you and the rest of the leadership team to actually make changes, don't survey your employees. However, even if there is a commitment, you also want to know whether you are able to make the changes. For example, if the survey shows that employees are unhappy with their pay, you may be unable to make any adjustments to the compensation plan. If this is the case, then do not ask any questions related to pay. We are not saying to avoid questions for which you do not want to know the answers. We are saying to avoid questions which you are unable to do anything about. There is a marked difference between these two.

- *When is the best time to survey employees?* If you are trying to make it on the many Great Places to Work or Best Places to Work surveys, consider the timing of those surveys. You do not want to over-survey employees. Also think about time of year. Are there big projects that are due? Are there holidays coming up which could affect timing? Do you have budget constraints that would prevent you from making certain changes in the current year? On the other hand, if you want to ask your employees about their benefits, then conduct the survey months before you undergo your benefits insurance renewals so you can incorporate any feedback into your renewal process.

- *How will results be communicated?* You need to share the findings of the survey with employees. Before starting the survey, have a plan as to how you will communicate the results and let employees know this plan. Ensure that managers are equipped to handle any questions. We recommend having the HR Business Partner in the room when managers are reviewing results with employees, especially at the department level. Managers need to not become emotional with the results. This is where self-awareness is key. If a manager gets mad at the team for the results of the survey or if they try to single out employees who they think may have answered the questions a specific way, you can throw trust and therefore loyalty out of the window.

- *What if completion rates are low for the survey?* In general, 100 per cent of employees will not complete the survey, especially in large organizations. That is okay. Even 90 per cent is a good number and will provide meaningful results. However, you need to be prepared if the completion rates are fairly low. This is a sign that engagement and morale may already be low. It may also mean that if you surveyed them in the past and nothing has changed, they could think *why even bother?* Lastly, low participation could mean that employees do not believe they will remain anonymous. Before starting the survey, think about whether you want respondents to remain anonymous. If the answer is no, then participation rates will be low. Do not make participation mandatory. But, if participation rates are low, take that as a sign and come up with a new plan to get the data you need to make the necessary changes.

- *Is an employee engagement survey the best, or only, way to get employee feedback?* Depending on what you are trying to measure, the answer may very well be no. For example, if there is an issue with a specific manager or if employees are close to walking out the door, an engagement survey will not help.

- *Should we consider other surveys?* With a diverse talent strategy, your actual workforce will be represented by more than just employees. As that mix changes, don't forget to get feedback from other groups adding value to your organization. Think about what might be important to know from them. It could be engagement related, or 'What's important to you?', or 'What do you like about doing work with us?'

Other sources of feedback

Companies are getting more innovative in creating opportunities for feedback. Traditional surveys, pulse surveys, and daily surveys about people's feelings and engagement are some of the common methods, but we are seeing an increased focus on executive exposure such as 'Coffee with the CEO' or rotating lunches with key leaders as other ways for people to just connect and listen. Often, as leaders' responsibility increases, they sense a decrease in personal connection to individuals. The CEO who used to know every employee's name and family, can be frustrated when they walk down the halls and see people they do not recognize. Looking for innovative ways to make and sustain personal connections between everyone within the organization, including key leaders who often get tied up in the boardroom, can prove invaluable to an organization. Plus, these touchpoints serve as an additional way to build that trust, which leads to engagement, which leads to loyalty. We encourage you to create these kinds of discussions and to go into them in an informal way; perhaps open with a brief update and set the stage to listen. Really hear and connect with people. Perhaps have a few targeted questions that you can use as prompts if people do not open up right away. This can also be a good place to leverage your HR advisor. They can help to both encourage meaningful discussion and be a partner in the accountability of doing something with what you learn from these forums. While it might seem challenging to create the time and space for this, it is well worth the investment.

Below are some questions you can use for those informal coffee or lunch chats. As mentioned before, if there are specific areas you would like to know about, customize the questions for your needs. If you are looking for a starting point, some of these questions could serve as ways to break the ice and open the door to deeper discussions.

SAMPLE QUESTIONS FOR CEO CHATS AND INFORMATION DISCUSSIONS

These work well for in-person/conversation-based surveys and discussion. They can also be adapted for online engagement surveys as appropriate.

General strategy questions:

- What is our company's mission/vision?
- What are your team's key priorities?
- In your opinion are we set up to achieve the strategy outlined by senior leaders?
- What holds us back from setting strategy or achieving our goals?

General culture questions:

- How would you describe the culture within the team or within the company?
- How might people outside our organization describe the culture?
- What is working well within our culture?
- What is not working well?

Leadership effectiveness questions:

- How would you describe the leadership team's style?
- What could we do to be more effective?
- Can you share some examples of leaders living the core values?
- How aligned do you think decision making is with our core values within the company?

Team dynamic questions:

- Do people behave in a way that fosters a climate of trust? How so?
- How does the team encourage healthy intellectual debate?
- Are you comfortable asking for feedback or help from leaders? From peers?
- Do team members consistently follow through on commitments?

Communication and transparency questions:

- How would you describe communication within our company (or within your team)?
- What are the barriers to more seamless communication or knowledge sharing?
- How do you get information you need to do your job?
- What information would help you do your job better?

Personal/getting to know you questions:

- How do you like to be recognized for a job well done?
- What keeps you coming back to work here every day?
- In your opinion, what can we do to ensure you feel supported by us?
- Do you enjoy coming to work? Why or why not?
- What is important to you in the work you do?

The questions above can also be adapted to hold these informal discussions as part of the onboarding and check-in process. For example, perhaps each quarter, all new hires are invited to a lunch or coffee with you and you can start to receive their input early. This allows you and the leadership team to take any action early, before things become a problem. When in person, remember to solicit feedback that they might not be comfortable sharing within a group. For example, if there is a leader that they are thinking of that does not model the core values, they may not want to say it in front of others. That said, it would be really valuable information for you to know. So encouraging people to stay after or to follow up separately is important. Make yourself available.

As you consider gathering feedback from your employees, consider whether the symptoms you may be seeing that are driving your effort to look at culture may not be the actual root cause of a less than desirable culture. For example, if on the survey employees provide feedback around their poor manager or the lack of adherence to the core values, these can often be symptoms of a larger problem, such as an issue in the management structure or a need for further development and training.

Are you and the team ready to really look at reality and face it head on? Sometimes it can be a relatively simple fix, such as creating more communication or dealing with an ineffective leader, but often it is not quite so simple or quick. Do you and the organization have enough commitment to creating a better outcome to stick with the heavy lifting? Do you have the necessary skills internally to help you navigate this process and affect change? As we mentioned in Chapter 3, this can be a great place to engage a highly skilled gig worker or consultant. Someone who can provide an external lens and help you navigate the engagement survey and feedback process and put an action plan in place. This is the work we routinely do with our clients and the benefit they have mentioned that an outside party brings is the ability to clearly see what actually is being said and done. Oftentimes as leaders you are mired in the day to day and your lens can become clouded. An external consultant can help ensure you are clearly seeing what needs to be done.

Depending on what you find in the feedback, creating a transparent path to meaningful change will be important. Feedback is like Pandora's box: once it's open, you can't close it without repercussions. If you want to build trust, do what you say, and say what you do once you open the box. Trust us, it is always better than trying to force it to stay closed.

CASE STUDY

A New-York based environmental non-profit client of ours asked us to take a deep dive into their culture. Their organization was traditional in many respects, but they wanted to break out of that mould and really be cutting edge and innovative. They knew that started with their culture and employees.

As we began interviewing employees and leaders, we found that every single one of them was tied to the mission and purpose of the organization, but they were all disheartened by the fact that the organization had routinely asked for their feedback and opinions through surveys but never once taken action.

As part of our debrief with the executive team, we mentioned this and stated the importance of communicating the new journey, why our organization was hired to assist, and how all employees would be part of the solution. In fact, we even presented this same exact information at the all-employee town hall meeting. Employees were energized and excited.

In the weeks that followed, we held focus groups and individual interviews with employees on values, management, culture, HR policies, etc. About six weeks after that town hall meeting, the executive team started making excuses as to why they could not continue with the plan and why only minimal changes, if any, were going to be implemented.

Fast forward six months, and we heard from numerous employees (current and former) that things only continued to get worse. This furthered the lack of confidence in leadership. Our biggest lesson learned from this particular experience was the need to pay attention to history and to gauge the commitment level of the executive team in affecting real change. It is an example of 'be careful what you ask for' if you are not prepared to really listen and create the necessary changes.

The simple art of listening

Everything we discussed above, whether feedback was provided through engagement surveys or informal conversations, requires listening. Employees want to feel heard. They want to know you care, as we mentioned before, and they want to see action over lip service. For leaders, listening is not only important in these large-scale events; it is especially important in the one-on-one meetings and moments. When leaders are good listeners, they build trust. In fact, according to a 2017 study, employees who felt their voices were heard were nearly five times more likely to feel engaged and empowered to do their best work.[2]

We are not saying that simply listening to employees is a sure-fire way to increase engagement and fix every problem. In fact, you do not have to agree with everything that is being said and it doesn't mean you have to implement every suggestion that is being provided by employees. However, emotional intelligence and self-awareness are necessary in order to be a good listener. When you make listening a priority, employees are also more open with ideas and ways to improve the business. If employees feel that they are being heard, they do not want to just talk about the culture, but ways to be innovative and achieve business priorities. On the other hand, if you aren't listening, then they will take their voice and those ideas to your competitor. Above all else, thank employees for their feedback. Let them know you appreciate their openness and ability to share. This sounds small but it goes a long way.

Engagement surveys and informal discussions are not the only way to take action and increase engagement.

Connecting skills to each employee

In Chapter 5, we talked about the skills necessary to succeed now and in the future. But defining the skills is just the beginning. It's important to connect those skills back to the employee's job, how those skills show up for the employee, and, if there are skills that the employee doesn't possess but should, there should be development opportunities for them to learn them. You then have to take these skills and communicate with employees about why they matter and connect them to your expectations and performance management process.

Self-fulfilling prophecies are real. You get what you expect. And in the case of organizations, you not only get what you expect, you get what you measure. After defining key skills, how are you integrating them into your HR policies and processes? Are individual contributors being promoted because they are good at their jobs and now they should manage people? Or are they being promoted because they possess the key competencies needed at the manager level? If you do not build an infrastructure that supports your key competencies, then your business could fail.

As leaders, you also need to communicate with employees and tell them what is expected in their roles, both for the actual job but also as a citizen of the organization. So often, we want to compare our employees to our kids. We often hear, 'My kids follow directions better than my employees,' or, 'Even my 10-year-old listens better than my direct reports'. This is perhaps one of the worst things we can do. Our employees are not children. They are adults and should be treated as such. Not only are they adults, but they are also fully capable individuals and valuable members of a team, not just a means to an end. If you treat your employees like children, they will act like children. If you treat them like adults, they will act like adults. It is a total self-fulfilling prophecy.

Remember all that talk about trust? Well, treating employees as adults starts with trust. Trust works both ways – you need to trust your employees *and* they need to trust you. As Gandhi once said, trust begets trust. In a 2016 survey of CEOs from around the world, PricewaterhouseCoopers found that 55 per cent of CEOs think that a lack of trust is a direct threat to the growth of their organization, up from 37 per cent just three years prior.[3] And according to *Great Place to Work*, a high-trust culture leads to a 50 per cent lower voluntary turnover.[4]

Once trust is established and expectations are clear, it is easier to empower your employees, give them autonomy over their work, allow them to make decisions, and provide them with guidance, resources, and feedback to help. However, this is not a place to micromanage employees. We can tell you that it is a sure way to have employees leave, rather than motivate and engage them.

Hold employees accountable for their decisions, but do not berate them if a decision or a solution they came to is not what you would have chosen. Often, leaders already have an answer or solution in mind when talking to their employees. Because of this, they cannot see that other solutions may exist, sometimes solutions that are better than the one they came up with. Allow employees to come to their own conclusions using facts, data, and experience to guide them. Your job is to ask questions and allow them to explain how they came to a specific solution or decision.

> **CULTURE QUOTE**
>
> Focus on the people side of business. Spend time, money, and energy on building leadership at all levels. When leadership is strong, employees are happy, and work gets done. Too often we focus on the metrics and do not pay attention to the people leading those who achieve the metrics.
>
> *Tacy Riehm, Founder, Leadership Consultant, Speaker and Executive Coach at Vos Consulting, LLC*

According to a 2018 *Forbes* article, there are three reasons why high performers are often miserable.[5] First, they often have the worst jobs. Second, their complaints are often ignored. Finally, low performers are not held accountable. We have worked for organizations where leaders knew they had a low performer and did nothing about it. The low performer continued to get paid, continued to take time off, continued to earn a bonus, and continued to get away with not doing a good job. As People and Culture (or HR), we heard many complaints from other team members that they felt undervalued, underappreciated, and were disengaged due to this unfair disconnect in standards. The low performer in this case is like the elephant in the room. Everyone knows he or she is there, but rather than remove them, everyone, including the leader, works around them.

CASE STUDY

Many years ago, Hema worked for a large, well-known Fortune 500 company. Performance reviews were done according to level (leaders, senior leaders, all employees, etc). While the general layout and guidance were the same on each form, the performance evaluation behaviours being assessed were all different. For example, leaders were measured on insight, their ability to energize, engage, coach and develop, among other things.

Senior leaders were measured on their ability to inspire the organization, develop and execute on strategy, and create an inclusive culture. While all other employees were measured on how well they understood the business environment, their initiative was in their ability to practise what they preached.

The differentiation was intentional to help people focus on the most important skills for their level of responsibility. This organization was a clear example of not only knowing the skills that were important to them at every level, but then holding everyone accountable for those skills. If you did not score well in any of the behaviours/areas, then there were opportunities to assist in developing those areas. No one was promoted to the next level until they had mastered the behaviours at their current level.

The most successful businesses today have active processes to support talent management. Integrated talent management processes look at performance, potential, capabilities, individual interest, and more, and use that information to inform job and project assignments in ways that are best for both the company and the individual employees. In addition to taking an active approach to talent management, engagement requires leaders and managers who actively think about the kinds of assignments their employees have and feel a sense of responsibility to be an advocate and shepherd to support people in their career. As a hint, remember those job descriptions we discussed in Chapter 3? Having incorrect, old or ineffective job descriptions is one way to disengage employees. If job descriptions are how employees are compensated in your organization, then leaders and managers should be reviewing the job descriptions to ensure they are accurate and clearly represent not only what is expected of the employee but what they are actually doing as well.

Ideal state for engagement

When you have a top performer, what are the causes of them becoming disengaged? Not feeling connected to their team or manager, not having meaningful work, and not being challenged to learn and grow. Remember: challenge is key to engagement. On the flip side, when people have the perfect combination of challenge, confidence, and interest, it is possible to enter an ideal state, often referred to as flow state.

Flow state is something that we strive for; sometimes this is referred to as being in the zone. This is when we are performing an activity and are fully immersed in a feeling of energized focus, full involvement, and enjoyment in the process of the activity. This is when employees will bring their discretionary effort to their roles. While it might be tempting to think this is only for athletes or artists, it is amazing when you can capture a team or broader organization with the majority of people working in a state of flow. When we do this, we see things that look like hyper focus, personal commitment, and graceful execution. Flow cannot happen without a certain amount of challenge or stretch. This is important to remember when assigning work and/or hiring people.

Measurement through metrics

Setting expectations and having goals and objectives is great. But remember, you also need to measure performance. Establish meaningful metrics for your organization and some general metrics that help tell the story, such as turnover. Perhaps a meaningful metric is to increase sales of a new product by 10 per cent or to obtain 15 per cent of all revenue from a new region you entered. Metrics help bring clarity to those performance expectations we talked about above.

Metrics should not be created in a vacuum. Include your employees in the process, ensuring you gain buy-in and alignment along the way. This also allows for clarity should those metrics not be met – everyone agreed and there were no surprises when it came time to measure performance.

Whatever the metric, just make sure it is something that can be measured, especially if there is a monetary bonus based on the achievement of that metric. Nothing ruins engagement more than setting a metric, telling employees their bonus will be based on it, and then either not measuring it or measuring it inaccurately.

Lastly, think about the metrics associated with your engagement survey. For example, as a leadership team, think about the metrics that are meaningful to help measure how your culture is doing. When communicating results and the action plan to employees, communicate the metrics. For example, if you scored a 70 per cent on overall engagement, let employees know it's good, but you are trying to achieve 90 per cent and will be doing these things to get there. Metrics aren't just important at an individual level, they are important at the organizational level as well.

Common pitfalls

When talking about engagement and motivation, there are some common pitfalls where leaders and organizations fall short. You will notice that none of these are about perks and benefits or compensation, they are all about leadership behaviours and awareness:

Getting caught up in having all the answers. With the best of intentions, many leaders feel pressured to have all the information and the exact right answers before they communicate. If you have all of the answers, then why bother having a leadership team, asking employees for their feedback or even giving others the appearance that they have a say? The undesired impact of this is that there is a lack of transparency which erodes trust in an organization and within a team. Leverage your experts and other leaders, who you hired for a reason!

Underestimating the impact of not communicating. This aligns with things we have referenced before, but just as leaders are often not aware of how visible their behaviour, or lack thereof, is to an organization, the same can be said of not communicating. Too often leadership teams wait to communicate. They try to get the message perfect or are waiting for additional information. Sometimes, they are delaying the inevitable because they are trying to drum up the leadership courage to share difficult news. Whatever the reason, the impact again is that people see what is happening, hear through the grapevine, make up stories on their own (that might be worse than the truth) and the trust and confidence in the leadership team is undermined... resulting in disengagement. Sometimes it is better to communicate what you know and let employees know that you don't have all of the answers just yet.

Forgetting that others do not have the same information you do. When you spend most of your days discussing the priority topics for your organization, it is easy to forget that others may not have been exposed to the majority of those conversations. Do not assume that everyone has all of the same information you do. More often than not, there are only a handful of employees that know the whole story. While you do not have to share everything, when involving other people in decisions, be sure they have relevant information.

Taking a 'nice' culture too far. We all want to work in an environment where people are treated with respect and are generally 'nice' to one another. What can happen is that this becomes an excuse to not deal directly with challenges or uncomfortable situations. Remember that being 'nice' to one person may actually not be nice to a large group of people if it means not dealing with underperformance or behavioural issues. Recognize that this has a huge connection to keeping a team motivated and engaged. High-performing teams do not want to be weighed down by someone who is not carrying their weight or contributing net positive impact.

Questions to ask

Before embarking on engagement surveys, informal chats, skills training, performance management, etc, turn the lens inward on your own team, and try to assess where you are today with regards to engagement and motivation. The box below outlines some questions to ask.

> **QUESTIONS TO ASK – ASSESSING ENGAGEMENT AND MOTIVATION**
> - When was the last time we did an engagement or 'perspectives' survey?
> - Have we taken action from the feedback we received? Why or why not?
> - Are there things that are significant to the organization that we have not communicated to all employees? Should we? When?
> - Do we need to take an active effort to build transparency and trust?
> - What information would help people do their jobs better and increase motivation towards common goals?
> - Are we hearing from all areas of the business? If not, which departments are the loudest and why? Which ones are the quietest?
> - What mechanisms do we have in place to get direct feedback at the executive level? Skip level meetings? One on ones?

Moving to action: what you can do next

There are countless ways to engage and motivate your employees that lead to truly exceptional organizational culture. There are many fundamental items to ensure that employees are bringing their entire discretionary effort to work. Below are a few ways you can start to move to action today:

Ask employees. When was the last time you conducted an engagement survey? If it has been a while, consider starting small and perhaps even having a cross-functional focus group help you. In addition to helping with the types of questions and breadth/depth of the survey, this group can also help implement any solutions and serve as champions for the organization throughout the process. Oh, did we mention this also serves as a huge engagement booster for the employees asked to participate in the focus group? Plus, these employees then talk to other employees about the work they are doing and how the organization is listening and wants to take action. Of course, there are also great external partners and technology solutions that are available should you want to send a survey out to a large population. Many of these providers will share best practices, sample questions, and even benchmark data that may be helpful as you design your method of asking your employee group.

Address the elephants in the room. Are there employees throughout your organization who are bringing others down, whether through their performance or attitude? Perhaps you may even have one or two on your team. Work with your HR team on coming up with a plan to address these employees. One idea is to take a look at performance reviews over the last year or two. Review the employees who have received the lowest scores and see if a pattern emerges. HR can also engage managers directly in this process to find out how employees are doing, if there has been any improvement, or if performance has declined. Whatever the approach, just be sure you do it in alignment with your organization's values. While removing these low performers will boost engagement, doing so in a disrespectful manner will further hurt motivation.

Find flow. Our lives are such that we are constantly on the go. And while we have all experienced a flow state, whether personally or professionally, we know the rush of excitement and alignment it can bring. Try to allow space on your calendar for creativity and strategy. Think of this as focused flow time. Allow your employees the ability to do this too. Some of the best ideas have come from organizations setting a day or two aside as hackathons, time when employees can focus and dive deep to come up with new products, new uses for old products, etc.

Lessons from the real world

What does culture have to do with engagement and motivation?

> Everything. You have one (culture), and it's either working for you or against you. Culture is the foundation of how a business operates day to day. Whether overtly stated or not, it provides people with the stakes in the ground, expectations for how to operate and act with each other, with partners and with customers. It gives evidence for what's rewarded and supported, or what isn't, and helps people decide if they

fit in and align with your company. Not defining it (culture), not driving it intentionally, and not using it as a way to connect strategy with execution is a big mistake that will cost you.

Charlie Piscitello, Chief People Officer at Acutus Medical, Inc

Final thoughts

High engagement and motivation can be the reason why top talent stays with your organization versus going to the competitor. Feedback from employees is a great way to see what engagement is actually like within your organization. But you need to be open and honest and really listen to what is being said. More so, you need to have a plan in place to take action. Partner with HR or an external consultant to help you develop a roadmap and plan. Even if your engagement is high today, what are you doing to keep it that way? Do not take it for granted.

Before we leave this chapter, take a few minutes to write down two to three key takeaways that you have with regards to your organization's ability to engage and motivate talent. Consider engagement surveys, other feedback channels, performance expectations and flow states. Think about areas you can improve upon as a leader with your own team. Looking at this list, next to each takeaway write down one action item that you will commit to doing to ensure your team and all employees remain committed to your organization.

What will you commit to doing?

Endnotes

1 Mahan, T *et al* (2019) 2019 Retention Report. Work Institute, https://info.workinstitute.com/hubfs/2019%20Retention%20Report/Work%20Institute%202019%20Retention%20Report%20final-1.pdf (archived at https://perma.cc/HFC8-5HYC)

2 SalesForce Research (2017) The impact of equality and values-driven business, https://c1.sfdcstatic.com/content/dam/web/en_us/www/assets/pdf/datasheets/salesforce-research-2017-workplace-equality-and-values-report.pdf (archived at https://perma.cc/YC5Q-B9HQ)

3 PwC (2016) Redefining business success in a changing world – CEO Survey, January, https://www.pwc.com/gx/en/ceo-survey/2016/landing-page/pwc-19th-annual-global-ceo-survey.pdf (archived at https://perma.cc/M5U4-5AQX)

4 Great Place to Work (2020) 9 reasons a high-trust culture means better business, https://www.greatplacetowork.com/business-case-poll (archived at https://perma.cc/D83B-3LL3)

5 Murphy, M (2018) 3 reasons why high performers are miserable, *Forbes*, 01 July, https://www.forbes.com/sites/markmurphy/2018/07/01/3-reasons-why-high-performers-are-often-miserable/#a12df1745fc0 (archived at https://perma.cc/W3HQ-UYZQ)

08

Total Rewards

Business leaders should be intentional about what culture they want. Culture doesn't happen in a vacuum – it starts with the mission, vision and values but there is a whole lot more. Culture is formed by the people you hire, promote, and choose to put in leadership. It's the written and unwritten policies of the organization, how and when decisions are made, how people treat each other, how communication flows, and ultimately what behaviours are rewarded, and which ones won't be tolerated. Be consistent. Be firm. People are smart enough to do the sniff test – what you put on a wall doesn't mean anything unless you and your team live up to them.

NAOMI WERNER, VICE PRESIDENT HUMAN RESOURCES AT OSSUR

Compensation. Benefits. Perks. Recognition. Personal and professional development.

These are all terms associated with how we reward our employees for their performance. Collectively, this can be called Total Rewards (or TR for short). At a high level, you can think of TR as a type of contract – in exchange for their time and experience, employees will receive pay, benefits, recognition, etc. Think about TR in your organization. What keeps your employees loyal? What role does the TR package play in your organization when it comes to attracting, retaining, engaging, and motivating talent? What objectives is your TR strategy trying to achieve? If you are unsure how to answer these questions, don't worry. We will take a much deeper dive into TR and the various components of TR that all organizations should consider.

Components of TR

How we reward our employees has changed dramatically over time. We went from offering decent pay and basic health coverage to free food and all expenses paid incentive trips. Nowadays, a good salary, health benefits, and even a corporate bonus are table stakes. Employees expect organizations to offer these and then some.

The umbrella of TR encompasses five areas:

- compensation;
- benefits;
- well-being;
- development: personal and professional growth opportunities (ie trainings);
- recognition: programmes that thank and recognize employees.

Compensation is both fixed and variable pay. This includes base salaries, bonuses and equity/stock options provided to employees tied to their overall contribution to their team, department, and organization. Compensation is generally the area CEOs believe their employees care about the most. In fact, studies have shown that 89 per cent of leaders believe their employees left their organization because of more money, yet data shows that 88 per cent of voluntary terminations are due to factors deeper than money.[1] Trust us when we say, employees value money, but not as much as or more than other cultural factors. A number of years back, Hema worked for an organization where she was responsible for TR, among other things. Managers would routinely go to her to ask for pay increases for their employees who were interviewing and getting job offers from other organizations. The managers were always convinced that the genesis to leave was driven by money. Occasionally, managers would go straight to the CEO, explain the situation, and obtain approval to provide ridiculous pay increases to employees in the hope that they would stay. This strategy was successful, for 30–60 days, then the employee would still inevitably quit and take another job offer.

Benefits are the other most common component we think of when we think TR. Benefits are the various insurance offerings, such as medical, dental, vision, life insurance, disability, etc. It also includes retirement plans such as pensions and qualified profit-sharing plans such as a 401k in the United States. But benefits also encompass various time-off and leave policies, such as vacation time, sick time, paid time off (PTO) and leaves of absence. This component of TR is broader than just the employee. It is about providing for families as well.

Well-being is not a traditional TR component. However, in recent years it has become a critical component for organizations who want to attract and retain the best of the best. Well-being is about the environment in which employees work. We are not only talking about the physical space, although that is a part of well-being. We are talking about the emotional and mental environment as well. When we hear the term 'toxic culture', well-being is what is affected. Perhaps there are a lot of cliques or groups, so the environment is not welcoming. Or perhaps employees are afraid of the leadership, so the environment lacks trust and openness. Other common elements of well-being include mental health, diversity, inclusion and belonging efforts (which we will cover in the next chapter), flexibility in work hours, meaningful work, employee wellness offerings (onsite gyms, cafeteria, etc) and Corporate Social Responsibility (which we will talk more about shortly). Due to COVID-19, well-being is shifting. For some employees who are still in an office setting, physical space is important. However, for those working remotely, feelings of isolationism, being overwhelmed and a lack of resources can all play into well-being.

Development is centred around personal and professional growth. This component encompasses the various opportunities available to employees to further their skills, increase competencies and contributions and advance in their careers as well. Elements of development include one-on-one meetings with leaders, coaching and mentoring opportunities, overseas assignments, tuition reimbursement, virtual and in-person training, and promotions just to name a few.

Finally, *recognition* encompasses both informal and formal programmes that show appreciation, gratitude, and acknowledgement for an employee's contribution to the organization and its culture. Some common examples of recognition can be service awards, core values awards as we mentioned earlier, and milestone achievement awards. One element to recognition is a general sense or culture of recognition. For example, does your organization celebrate successes and accomplishments or are they considered *par for the course* and part of the job? We can tell you that a culture of appreciation goes a long way. A simple *thank you* can help.

The role of TR in designing an exceptional organizational culture

TR is a complicated yet integral part of building an amazing and long-lasting culture. Think about the various components of TR as levers that can be pulled and adjusted based on the desired outcome. Let's take incentive bonuses as an example. A technology client of ours discovered that their sales incentive bonuses were rewarding employees based on the number of sales. This sounds completely normal. However, employees were doing whatever it took to secure the sale, including leaving out critical information that would help the customer make a more informed decision. When we discovered this, we immediately knew we had to change the incentive plan. While the original intent was not to omit information or be deceitful, the unintended consequence was much different. After months of work, we amended the plan to still compensate for sales, but we added additional components tied to the organization's core values and compliance. In order to receive the full bonus potential, employees needed to not only complete sales, but do so in a manner that was aligned with the culture the organization wanted to build.

When done correctly, an organization's TR strategy and philosophy reinforce what the organization truly values. You reward and recognize the behaviours and actions that are most meaningful to the organization; behaviours and actions that should be aligned with the organization's core values. The exchange of what an employee receives for their contribution is central to defining the culture of an organization – if you contribute x, you will receive y.

If you want to better understand what a company values and what they expect from their employees, look at their TR strategy. Take a moment to think about your TR strategy. What does it say about your organization and what you value? How does that align with your culture? How does it align with what your employees say is important to them? If you do not know your organization's TR philosophy, find out. Much like the EVP from Chapter 6, all organizations have a TR philosophy, whether formal or informal. This philosophy also is important for boards of directors, who want to ensure invested capital is rewarding the right contributions and behaviours.

While all organizations have (or should have) elements of all five TR components, not all components are created equal. For example, for start-up organizations who are trying to build a strong culture but who may not have a lot of available cash, base pay can be lower and benefits may not be as robust, but well-being, development and even recognition are emphasized, as is equity or ownership in the organization. At this stage, it is more about an individual's contribution to the greater organization and succeeding as one team. Perhaps for more established companies, fixed pay is more important. Be sure you understand your TR philosophy and levers in the context of your organizational stage.

As the war for talent continues, we have seen organizations get creative with their TR offering – perks that are considered unique or special – in order to attract the type of talent they are looking for. We are not here to tell you about the type of compensation you should offer your employees, or whether Starbucks should deliver every day at 3 pm to avoid the afternoon 'lull' many employees find themselves in. Creating an exceptional organizational culture is not as much about the *types* of rewards that you offer as much as it is about the *meaning* of the rewards that you offer. In today's world, we also need to consider Total Rewards outside the traditional constraints of 'for employees only' and think about what kinds of offerings may be important as we look to attract talent of different kinds.

Personalized rewards

For a moment, think about an entry-level employee, perhaps someone early in their career. They do not earn a lot of money and what they do earn needs to go towards rent, fuel, insurance, and food. Once those expenses are paid, there is not much left over from their monthly paycheck. Now, think about a senior leader. Someone who has enough discretionary income at the end of the day to own multiple vehicles and take three to four large vacations annually.

Now think about how each would react to receiving a $50 gas gift card. This reward is probably more meaningful to the entry-level employee with less (or even no) discretionary income than it is to that senior leader. While this is an oversimplified example, the point is that each employee values something different based on their personal circumstances.

It sounds simple and logical enough. We all know that we each value different things and may not find the same level of meaning in various rewards. The truth is the one-size-fits-all approach was, and still is, extremely common. One such area where this standardization does not work is with salary reviews. Employees do not want to wait until the one time of year when your organization does salary reviews. Yet, 91 per cent of respondents in a rethinking rewards survey stated they only do salary reviews one time a year.[2] If organizations really want to attract, retain, and engage top talent, a standardized TR package will not do the trick. Employees want more than just base pay and benefits.

Rewards are meant to incentivize people and motivate them to continue doing their best work. And what motivates each of us is different. This is where the concept of personalized rewards comes into play. While some of your Total Rewards may be more difficult to personalize (compensation, health benefits, etc), other benefits can easily be personalized. These rewards are tied to performance and can include recognition programmes, career milestones/achievements, promotions, and even a great performance review.

A few years ago, Hema was speaking on a panel about how it was becoming increasingly tougher for organizations to recruit and retain top talent and how organizations were realizing the importance and value of recognizing and rewarding their employees. One of the panellists, a CHRO for a well-known biotech company, shared that, in order to truly understand what each of his employees wanted (what motivates them, what excites them to do better, and what their expectations are about rewards), he sat down with each and every one of them and asked them. Can you imagine what this must have been like for him? Interview after interview. Week after week, until all 250 employees had been interviewed. However, as he stated, this was one of the most fulfilling and meaningful experiences he had in his career to date. He was able to really understand his employees and get to know them on a deeper and personal level. He learned about whose kids were into what sports. Or which employee loved fostering puppies. Or who took care of their parents and delivered groceries to their home each week.

These interviews became the basis for the organization's new rewards and recognition programme. Gone were the days of generic gift cards. What followed was a points-based system allowing employees to earn points through various recognition awards and use those points to choose from various rewards available, all built with the employees' feedback in mind. Rewards included gift cards (for gas, groceries, pet stores, etc), company logo merchandise, various experiences (jet skiing, skydiving, rock climbing) and many more. This approach allowed employees to spend their points when they wanted to and on what they wanted to. But, more importantly, employees felt heard. Think back to Chapter 7 and what we mentioned about really listening and taking action. This is a prime example of what action looks like to increase engagement.

Now, we are not saying that you have to go out and interview all of your employees, although if you do not have a lot of employees, it may be a worthwhile exercise. What we are saying is that it is important to understand that rewards should not be a one-size-fits-all approach.

If rewards are to be used to actually reward performance or a success or a milestone, then they should be meaningful to the individual receiving them. They should also be aligned with your organizational culture.

> **CULTURE QUOTE**
>
> Beware the echo chamber. If your 'source of truth' on organizational culture is your management team and your HR leader, you are missing the complete story. Create as many feedback loops and monitoring mechanisms as is reasonable. Our cross-departmental culture committee has been a large part of our success during COVID/work from home. We have a group of dedicated employees who give us feedback as we rapidly roll out new policies and procedures and provide ideas and insight into the health of our culture and employee base. Be careful when setting company values. Values are the biggest ingredient in a company's culture. If you pick values that you wish the company embraced but don't, it will be seen as insincere or tone-deaf at best and hypocritical at worst. Organizational culture is organic. In small businesses, each time you add an employee, you alter the culture. Organizations that embrace this truth will be able to spot positive and negative changes faster and course correct as needed.
>
> *Ken Ruggiero, Chairman and Chief Executive Officer at Goal Solutions*

A personalized strategy can even be offered for compensation. For example, one European consulting firm allows new employees, at time of hire, to choose between salary or stock options, higher pay or an extra week of vacation, or increased bonus opportunity or higher salary increases.[3] At the onset, employees are choosing rewards that are more meaningful to them. Strategies such as this are less common, but this consulting firm is definitely considered a first mover in the arena of personalized rewards. Plus, as the decision is up to the employee, there is less disagreement or negotiation because the choice is theirs.

Employee benefits are another area where the personalization strategy can work. We are not talking about the specific benefits and creating individual plans for each employee. We are talking about the organization's contribution to the premium for these benefits. In a traditional benefits strategy, the organization pays a set or defined percentage or dollar value towards employee and dependent coverage. For example, if an organization offers two medical plan options, the employer may pay 100 per cent of the employee-only cost for the cheapest plan and 50 per cent of the dependent cost. The more expensive option is considered a buy-up, where employees have to pay extra out-of-pocket for the enhanced coverage. In addition, the organization may offer one or two dental insurance options, one vision option and a plethora of additional and voluntary benefits, like pet insurance. One strategy that can be used to personalize employee benefits is to consider providing employees with a pool of money. For example, instead of the percentage method outlined above, an organization can provide employees with a set dollar value they can then apply towards their benefits. Maybe this number is $8,000 per year. At time of open enrolment, employees can choose how they use their money. Perhaps they enrol in dental, vision and pet insurance and forego medical. Or maybe they enrol in medical only. Whatever the selection, they are able to choose the benefits that are most meaningful to them. If they do not spend the entire $8,000 they don't receive it in cash. This is not about spending as little as possible and banking the rest. It is about being able to tailor your benefits package to your circumstances. In our experience, when organizations implement such a strategy, they expand their benefit offerings to include ID theft protection, legal protection, financial counselling, long-term care, student loan refinancing programmes, a virtual assistant, chore and errands assistance, etc. Honestly, the list is endless!

Reward strategies that are agile and personalized create a culture where employees feel valued for their individual accomplishments and not just the team accomplishments. Plus, employees are more motivated and engaged because the rewards they are working towards are tailored to their needs. The possibilities for personalizing rewards are great. However, the true test is how many organizations are willing to throw the standard rewards methodology out the window and opt for a new and innovative approach. Although we are seeing more cutting-edge and start-up organizations leaning towards this path, long-term change will take time.

What do your rewards say about your organization?

Regardless of the reward strategy you use, the types of Total Rewards you offer, and why you offer them, says a lot about your organization. Take Google. They offer free food, a fully equipped gym, onsite haircuts, laundry, dry cleaning facilities, an onsite medical clinic, and a very generous maternity and parental bonding leave plan. While some of these benefits sound more like Google's way to make employees stay onsite, and at work longer, others show that Google cares about employee health and well-being. If you think about your rewards, everything you offer your employees, what do your rewards say about your organization? Do your rewards effectively communicate who you are, and are these offerings aligned with your organization's core values?

Alignment with core values

As we have previously mentioned, your core values should not just be words on a wall. They should be embedded into every fibre of your organization, including the types of Total Rewards you offer employees. For example, if one of your core values is *Fiercely Authentic*, would employees looking at their TR package be able to say that what they are offered to help motivate, engage, and retain them really does align with this particular core value? If not, you may want to think a bit more closely about the personalized rewards strategy we mentioned above.

One place we often see a misalignment between a benefit being offered and an organization's core values is around bereavement leave. Perhaps your organization's policy is that bereavement leave is three days and only covers the passing of immediate family. What you are saying is that, regardless of your organization's core values and regardless of who your employees have lost, they have three days to grieve the loss and move on. We don't know about you, but that sounds cold and harsh.

Many organizations are realizing that the old and stale bereavement leave policy does not effectively and accurately represent who they are as an organization. In fact, the term *bereavement leave* is being replaced with grief leave and companies like Mastercard and Facebook are offering a generous 20-day grief leave. Why? Because these organizations realize that work is not top of mind when you have lost someone close to you. These organizations also know that by allowing their employees extra time, they are living true to their core values (trust and acting with integrity and respect for Mastercard and focusing on impact for Facebook). Can you imagine the level of loyalty and engagement employees would feel once they are back at work, knowing their organization cared so deeply about them?

When thinking about your core values in relation to Total Rewards, consider equity. As we have already mentioned, what each person values is different. Due to this, how fair or just someone finds a particular reward is really based on how they value that reward. In much the same way, organizations must consider equity in the value of rewards based on the various life stages of an employee. If your organization claims to be inclusive and even uses this term as part of the employee value proposition, your Total Rewards and associated policies had better reflect that.

Let us explain. About six years ago, innovative, cutting-edge organizations were looking to expand their maternity and paternity benefits. This expansion was not just occurring with large tech companies, but also smaller start-ups, who competed for talent with those larger tech companies. Organizations were providing full pay for up to 12 months for both maternity and paternity leave. While this benefit was great and deeply valued for those just starting their families or for the new parents, what about the employees who were at a stage in their life where they were caring for a sick parent or other family member? Or what about the employee who needed to be out of work due to a medical procedure? Was their financial stability and peace of mind not as important?

While we all want to say, 'no, of course not', the truth is there is a lack of inclusivity in leave policies, the types of policies that allow employees to take time off work to care for themselves and their family members. We talk about this because we were guilty of it too. When we worked for a start-up a number of years back, we jumped on the overly generous maternity and paternity policies bandwagon in order to attract the talent we were looking for. A year after we rolled out the generous policy, we pulled it back and adjusted the length of time moms and dads could stay out with full pay and reallocated some of the money towards other leave policies. For example, if employees needed to be out of work due to their own medical issue or to take care of a sick family member, we provided them with full pay for eight weeks. While we anticipated backlash (because no one wants to roll out a policy only to change course just one year in), we were pleasantly surprised by the feedback. Employees were grateful that we expanded the benefit to be more inclusive and they felt that it spoke more to who we were as an organization – one that took care of *all* employees, and not just some of them.

Alignment with business strategy

In addition to aligning your rewards with your values, consider your business strategy. Again, consider your Total Rewards programme. Is it clear what objectives are important to your organization and how your rewards align to the overarching strategy? If the answer is no, do your employees know what is expected of them and how their work fits into the overall goals of the organization?

A 2018 study conducted by Deloitte found that high-performing organizations are six times more likely to use data to better understand employee preferences and are also focused on best fit versus best practice and align Total Rewards with business goals.[4] Here, best fit is more about taking a look at what your organization needs to accomplish and the type of talent your organization wants to attract and retain in order to accomplish those goals. It is not about what your competition offers and matching that or paying at the 50th percentile. What works for one organization may not work for another. Create something that is unique to your organization and then ensure your tangibles (ie base salary, bonus, etc) and intangibles (ie professional development, quality of work, etc) align with what your organization needs to accomplish.

Communicating how the TR strategy is aligned with the business objectives is important. You may already be doing this within your organization when you cascade goals. For example, there may be a corporate goal to create a new product. At the executive level, you assign this goal to one of your direct reports, perhaps the Chief Strategy Officer. Your Chief Strategy Officer then cascades pieces of the goal down to his or her team and so on. Each of these objectives is weighted and is taken into consideration during merit and bonus time. This example also becomes cross-functional. If creation of that new product requires new hires, then a portion of this goal should also appear on your CHRO's performance review. The point is that all individual objectives that determine an employee's bonus or merit or even promotion opportunities should connect back to the corporate goals.

Pay mix

Lastly, while alignment with core values and the business strategy are important, so is your pay mix in determining what your Total Rewards actually say about your organization. Pay mix is the ratio of your base salary to target incentives. For example, a 70/30 pay ratio means 70 per cent of an employee's on-target earnings (OTE) is from a fixed base salary while 30 per cent is from a bonus or other variable pay. This pay mix can differ by role within your organization; usually sales roles have higher variable pay. This can also be the case with executives. Your pay mix speaks to the level of risk an employee will be signing up for when they join your organization. If there is too much at stake with variable pay, they will weigh the difficulty of the position, other offers they may have received, and ultimately, they may not feel comfortable. If there is not enough at stake, high performers may not feel motivated to bring their best every day. Review your current pay mix by level and for both sales and non-sales positions.

Use the data to help you determine whether employees are encouraged to be innovative and motivated or whether they are becoming complacent in their positions.

The truth is, rewards and what you offer employees say a lot about how you value and care for them. But rewarding employees goes deeper than just what they can gain financially and through personal and professional development and recognition. Employees also want to know how organizations contribute to their community and those not directly associated with the organization.

Beyond pay and benefits

The make-up of the workforce is changing. The Baby Boomers are retiring at a rapid rate and Millennials will comprise 75 per cent of the workforce by 2025.[5] As the demographics of employees change, what they value changes as well. While newer generations are still concerned with pay and wanting to feel financially secure, pay is no longer the main deciding factor when choosing which organization to join. In fact, in a 2016 survey, 75 per cent of Millennials stated they would take a pay cut to work for a socially responsible company.[6] Think about that for a second. Employees are more concerned with the behaviour and actions of their organization than they are their own paycheck. So, what does *socially responsible* even mean?

Corporate Social Responsibility, or CSR for short, is a business model that helps organizations be more socially accountable to all stakeholders and to the greater community at large. The overarching goal is not just to the bottom line of the organization, but to creating a better and more productive world for the long term. CSR strategies generally fall into four buckets: philanthropic, environmental, labour practices, and volunteerism, as outlined in Figure 8.1. Depending on the industry, employees may be concerned with one or two of these areas rather than all four.

In Chapter 6, we talked about Unilever and their EVP. Unilever makes CSR part of their EVP. They have recognized that employees want to feel good about the organization they work for and that they

FIGURE 8.1   CSR categories

Philanthropic: Strategies that align with and support philanthropic causes.

Environmental: Strategies that decrease an organization's carbon footprint.

Labour Practices: Strategies that create ethical and fair labour practices at all levels of an organization.

Volunteerism: Strategies that allow employees to give back to the community.

also want to feel and be part of something that is bigger than themselves. Again, right on the careers page of the website is a section called Sustainable Living, with a message that reads, 'Our vision is a new way of doing business – one that delivers growth by serving society and the planet.' The site goes into their approach to CSR and even provides a sustainable living report. In fact, Unilever's CSR strategy checks all four buckets: philanthropic, environmental, labour practices, and volunteerism.

We do not think that organizations need to spend millions of dollars on CSR or even completely change their business model. What we do believe is that being part of an organization that contributes to the greater community is also often perceived as a reward. This means that organizations need to consider rewards that highlight corporate citizenship. In doing so, leaders are putting their organizational culture, ethos, and values at the forefront. Plus, employees are more engaged and fulfilled.

Some companies are feeling compelled to create company policies that make a community statement. One example here is with the COVID-19 pandemic. Many employers, even without federal funding, decided not to negatively impact employees during the mandated shelter in place orders. While not every business had the cash to make this decision, we saw public companies enact this policy despite revenue impact, whether known or unknown. They encouraged employees to donate time or items in their communities, partnered with other agencies to contribute to local efforts, and invested in their employees' well-being and mental health. While CSR strategies and having a community-minded approach does not alleviate leaders from the responsibility of making prudent financial decisions, it is becoming a valued expectation for many employees as they determine what kind of organization they want to be part of.

Incorporating CSR strategies into your daily operations is not as difficult or time-consuming as it seems. Years ago, Hema worked for an organization that, once a year, would shut down so employees could spend the day volunteering. A committee was formed and this committee's task was to find five different volunteer opportunities (ie assisting at the food bank, beach clean-up, etc), then every employee would sign up for the opportunity that was most meaningful to them. Because this was companywide, the added benefit was meeting and getting to know people from outside of your own department. A few years after this volunteer day started, the organization started a foundation to give grants to local nonprofits so they could continue their mission. Employees felt more connected to the organization based on their philanthropy, plus the organization attracted other socially responsible employees, therefore cultivating a culture of corporate good.

Common pitfalls

The world of Total Rewards is constantly evolving. As employee preferences change, organizations try to keep pace in order to attract and retain top talent. A one-size-fits-all approach is no longer the answer. Completely starting over and throwing your current TR programme away is not beneficial either. There are definitely some pitfalls to be on the lookout for when trying to create TR programmes that speak to who you are as an organization and that take into account employee preference. Below are a few of the most common:

Designing TR programmes focused on some, and not all, stakeholders. We have seen organizations have a knee-jerk reaction when one or two of their high-performing employees leave due to money. What ends up happening is an ad hoc incentive plan is created designed to pay employees based on short-term objectives without taking into account the long-term interests of customers, investors, or other stakeholders. These programmes are generally just a band-aid solution and they can cause more harm than good.

Spending too much money on TR programmes. There is a common misconception that the best reward programmes cost a lot of money. That you have to spend a lot to make a difference. The truth is you absolutely do not. If you are spending money on rewards that are not contributing to your culture, to employee engagement and retention and which are not aligned with your core values, we would ask, 'why are you offering them at all?' Small gestures can have a big impact. A thank you card or public recognition is sometimes all it takes.

Not seeking expert advice. It is very easy to get a TR strategy wrong. Unwinding it can be extremely difficult, not to mention the harm it can do to the culture in the process. Seeking guidance from an expert in this area can provide you with valuable insights into potential reward options that you may not have initially considered. Plus, an expert can help steer you away from common mistakes.

Not understanding history. When new leaders take over, it can be easy to want to try to disregard previous programmes and policies that had been used in the past and start over with what you think is best. While you may have designed an amazing TR programme at a previous organization, do not assume that it will work for your new organization. Seek to understand what rewards were offered at your organization prior to your arrival and why they worked or did not work. You do not want to repeat history if it was a bad experience. A financial services company Hema worked for a few years back ran into this issue. Hema was asked to create a rewards programme for financial advisors who were not employees of the organization. There was a big push to offer the advisors benefits, such as medical insurance. Hema asked a lot of questions around whether anything like this had ever been done before and, if so, if it was successful. The short answer was it had been tried before and lasted for two years before it was dismantled. The reasons for cancelling the programme were valid, but the financial advisors didn't respond positively when a benefit was taken away, especially after only a short time. If Hema had not asked the questions, the organization would have repeated history.

Making rewards transactional. How do you communicate merit increases or bonus awards to employees? Do you send a generic email to all recipients stating the pay day they will see their money? Oftentimes, administration of TR programmes can be transactional and come across as cold or not caring. Use instances like merit increases, bonuses, open enrolment for benefits, etc as a time to really communicate with your employees all the wonderful things your organization offers, how employees fit into the big picture, and reiterate the culture you are trying to create. Do not waste these opportunities! Also consider Total Rewards statements. These statements are a really easy way to show your employees, and their families, the benefits that your organization provides.

Questions to ask

Your Total Rewards strategy should show a clear connection between business objectives/business strategy and how you reward employees. The box below provides questions for you to ask yourself and members of your HR Team in order to determine the true impact of your TR strategy.

QUESTIONS TO ASK – ASSESSING THE IMPACT
OF YOUR TR STRATEGY

- What are we trying to achieve with our TR strategy? Does our current programme achieve those goals?
- What kind of workforce do we need to achieve our business objectives?
- What do the people who we want to attract and retain value the most?

- What rewards (monetary and non-monetary) do we need to offer/stop offering to truly become an employer of choice and attract high-performing top talent?
- Which elements of our programme are we willing to get creative with and think outside of the box on?
- How do our employees value their benefits? Do we need to make trade-offs to emphasize one element of the programme over another?
- How will we ensure our TR strategy stays current and relevant?
- As we expand our talent strategy into differentiated talent and the elastic workforce, what considerations do we need to have related to talent working with us that are not direct employees?

Moving to action: what you can do next

A strong, aligned, and connected Total Rewards strategy not only says a lot about who your organization is, but it also lets employees (and future employees) know what you value.

Take inventory. Before you start asking employees what they value, figure out where you are today. Take inventory of everything you offer that could be labelled Total Rewards. Remember, this is deeper than just compensation. Write down the types of rewards you give out. For example, if you have a core values champion award, what reward do you provide winners? If you have top sales awards, what do the winners receive? Do you offer service awards or other tenure-based rewards? Birthday celebrations? Then think about some of the 'extras'. Things like free food, onsite gym, and trainers. Do not forget about benefits like medical insurance, life insurance, and various leave policies. The goal is to write everything down, so you know exactly what you offer and where you are starting from.

Prioritize. Not all of these items have equal weight and equal importance. Some of the items may not be able to be changed immediately anyway. For example, medical benefits renew annually for most organizations. Rather than making mid-year plan changes, you may have to wait until your renewal cycle comes back around.

Review your list closely and group items together. Consider the following categories to help you: compensation, benefits, time off, perks (eg free food), and recognition. Your organization may have others, depending on what you offer. Once grouped, start prioritizing what is most important/what can't wait and what can. This will give you a good idea of where to focus.

Come up with a plan. Once you have your priorities in order, think of next steps. Remember, this should not be an activity you, or your team, does in a silo. This should be a cross-functional/cross-departmental plan. HR often leads these efforts and works with leaders and other employees. Depending on the size of your organization, we recommend assembling a project team of stakeholders. This should be a group of employees representing different levels and departments within the organization. They should be in good standing with your organization and also be models for the core values (in Chapter 6, we talked about a culture committee). This is a great place to pull in cultural ambassadors. Whatever plan you choose, just make sure you set a realistic due date for a revamped rewards programme and that you communicate!

Lessons from the real world

What role does Total Rewards play in organizational culture?

> The Total Rewards philosophy *and practice* sets the tone of the organization's culture. The philosophy isn't an aspirational goal, it should be reflective of how the company values individuals and thus their pay. The rewards package offered and accepted by a person for a new role sets expectations for how the culture really plays out in an organization. If the culture is one of fairness and respect you are most likely going to find that reflected in pay packages as well. Unfortunately, in some companies, management allows inconsistent implementation of the philosophy or decides it doesn't really matter and this results in distrust and inequities in all areas, not just pay.
>
> *Cathy McCutcheon, Vice President Compensation and Benefits at Ingram Micro*

People seek meaningful work and look for meaningful rewards. The design of your Total Rewards programmes can differentiate an organization and keep employees continuously engaged and contributes to a positive culture.

Steve Weiss, Director of Compensation at Mitchell International

From your experience, what is the number one aspect of Total Rewards that employees value the most?

Cash is always king, although health insurance has moved up fast over the past few years due to the focus on the Affordable Care Act and concerns about COVID-19.

Cathy McCutcheon, Vice President Compensation and Benefits at Ingram Micro

Tough to pick one as it really depends on organization and employee type. I probably wouldn't have said this 5+ years ago and not all employees value it but a strong benefits (health and welfare) programme really puts a lot of employees at ease; I have seen weak benefits programmes cause lots of noise, disengagement, and allow employees to have no regrets about leaving voluntarily. Since it is so difficult and costly in 2020 for employers to provide strong benefits programmes, having a strong and competitive benefits programme differentiates an organization from others. You notice I do not have base salary or bonuses (cash) valued as highly since, rightly or wrongly, I feel they are more 'expected' and 'assumed' by the employee. Employees will likely not even join an organization if cash is not competitive. I have seen organizations get a lot of bang for their buck from flexible recognition programmes that enable frequent recognition up and down the organization – peer to peer, manager to subordinate, executives to all. Non-cash recognition from peer to peer is sometimes the most rewarding and engaging for lots of employees, especially now in times of tight budgets. This can really differentiate one organization from others and adds a lot of goodwill (karma); I feel organizations can get a lot of value from them IF they support and communicate them.

Steve Weiss, Director of Compensation at Mitchell International

What do you think will be an important benefit or perk in the future?

Most true perks have gone away due to tax laws and proxy disclosure rules; however, COVID-19 has caused most companies to relook at their past practices regarding remote work and flexibility. I think the most important perk in the future will be flexibility. This is the acknowledgement by the company that there may be days during the week that you won't be available during regular business hours or will need to be out of the office while they trust you to still get your work done. Since this isn't a benefit that can be purchased through a benefit portal, it will require significant change in management style, communication and understanding that some managers will embrace and others will struggle with.

Cathy McCutcheon, Vice President Compensation and Benefits at Ingram Micro

Flexibility. Flexibility to work whenever, wherever. Since so many people have worked remotely with success during the pandemic, we're starting to wonder if employees need to be in the workplace each day. This opens up doors to relocate to lower-cost communities, which is definitely a selling point. Working parents are starting work early and work late to accommodate mid-day disruptions because of younger kids at home. Many roles are global, so you're not working in the same time zone anyway. Why not give them this flexibility if they are available for key meetings, connect with people readily through video, and they get their job done? The accountability is on the person working remotely to demonstrate that they are getting the work done so they can continue to have this perk.

Naomi Werner, Vice President Human Resources at Ossur

Final thoughts

Total Rewards strategies and programmes are a way to showcase your culture and core values. When designed and communicated effectively they are an important tool for CEOs and HR Teams to attract, retain, engage, and motivate top talent. In order for organizations to be true employers of choice, they need to tap into what employees are looking for, which is deeper than just money. As a CEO, it is critical to understand that throwing money at a problem doesn't solve it. As an HR leader, it is essential to be able to communicate the various TR levers at your disposal and utilize those levers to create a high-performing culture.

Take a few minutes to write down two or three key takeaways from this chapter with regards to your organization's TR programme. What rewards are working well? Which programmes could use some work? Does your TR strategy accurately convey who you are as an organization and who you want to be? Now, review what you wrote and next to each takeaway write down one action item that you will commit to doing to ensure your TR strategy represents the culture you want to create.

What have you committed to do?

Endnotes

1 Branham, L (2013) The 7 hidden reasons employees leave, *Keeping the People Inc*, https://leadershipbeyondlimits.com/wp-content/uploads/2013/06/WhyPeopleLeave-Branham.pdf (archived at https://perma.cc/M4RJ-89H8)

2 Agarwal, D *et al* (2018) The rise of the social enterprise – 2018 Deloitte global human capital trends, *Deloitte*, https://www2.deloitte.com/content/dam/insights/us/articles/HCTrends2018/2018-HCtrends_Rise-of-the-social-enterprise.pdf (archived at https://perma.cc/UU82-YNSE)

3 Ibid.

4 Bersin Insights Team (2018) High-impact total rewards survey, *Bersin, Deloitte Consulting*, https://www2.deloitte.com/content/dam/Deloitte/ca/Documents/audit/ca-audit-abm-scotia-insights-from-impact-2018.pdf (archived at https://perma.cc/DN2U-8SJU)

5 Pelosi, P (2018) Millennials want workplaces with social purpose. How does your company measure up? *Talent Economy*, 20 February, https://www.chieflearningofficer.com/2018/02/20/millennials-want-workplaces-social-purpose-company-measure/ (archived at https://perma.cc/7AXJ-NV3Q)

6 Cone Communications (2016) Three-quarters of millennials would take a pay cut to work for a socially responsible company, 02 November, https://www.conecomm.com/news-blog/2016-cone-communications-millennial-employee-engagement-study-press-release (archived at https://perma.cc/E54W-CHCJ)

09

Diversity, inclusion, and belonging

I'd ask a question first: 'How bad do you want it?' Okay, maybe two: 'How hard do you want to work to achieve it, and over how many years?' Growing a strong, consciously designed organization of humans who act cohesively, contributing voluntarily year after year beyond what is asked is like being a forester. You have to think way ahead. It will take many years to make progress, and if you're starting from a poor position then there will be difficult people decisions to make before you can even start planting. And, like foresters who deal with living things that last hundreds, even thousands of years, it can't be about you. It's about the people whose lives you will affect long after you've hung up your hoe.
STAN SEWITCH, VICE PRESIDENT, GLOBAL ORGANIZATION DEVELOPMENT AT WD-40 COMPANY

Before we dive too deep into this chapter, we want to first align around definitions. Diversity, Inclusion, and Belonging (or DI&B for short) are often inseparable when discussing this topic. But they are three distinct things.

From our experience, diversity tends to be about characteristics and traits that make people unique. This is more than just skin colour or ethnicity. This is also about experiences, thoughts, and perspectives that make each one of us unique. Inclusion is more about making people feel welcome through societal norms and behaviours. In a work setting, inclusion is about treating all employees fairly, equitably, and respectfully, and making sure employees have equal access to opportunities and resources necessary to be effective contributors. Belonging is about having a work environment in which everyone feels that they belong and are part of the team. Studies show that belonging is something that is important to employees when choosing a place to work, as they want to feel an affinity for the company they work for and for the team they work with.

It is likely that there are many more ideas coming up for you as you think about these concepts. It is true that you can't simplify all the meaning of diversity, inclusion and belonging into a simple paragraph; we just want to set the stage with some common understanding to launch into it. Now that we've done that, let's dive in.

DI&B is not a quota

For many years, organizations simply measured diversity, and in this case, diversity was all about workplace representation. In the United States, most HR leaders have probably heard of the Equal Employment Opportunity survey (EEO-1) required for all private organizations with more than 100 employees and all federal contractors with more than 50 employees. The EEO-1 is a self-reported survey categorizing employees based on race/ethnicity, gender, and job category. The final survey is filed with the US Equal Employment Opportunity Commission (EEOC) which analyses employment patterns to ensure representation of women and minorities within organizations, industries, and regions. The goal of the EEO-1 is to 'show' diversity; to meet a quota by checking a box to say, 'Yes, we have equal representation'.

This is an extremely limited view and one that framed a perspective for many people that some companies might not hire the best person for the job due to an effort to meet quotas. The goal of the EEO-1 is not to determine whether organizations are providing equal access to opportunities for women and minorities once hired. It does not look at inclusion or belonging at all. And certainly, the EEO-1 does not begin to capture the truly diverse population that exists among our employees as you look beyond the specific demographics included in that report. This is merely about workforce representation and compliance. It has nothing to do with inclusive people strategies or bringing out the best in all of your people.

While the EEO-1 served a purpose for many years, to forward-thinking, innovative organizations whose cultures are strong, it remains a check in the box, a legal requirement they must complete if they meet the criteria. For these organizations, DI&B is ingrained into who they are and how they work; not for the sake of a report, but because they are committed to having the best teams possible and bringing out the best in them. These are the organizations where DI&B initiatives are built into every facet of the employee cycle (from recruiting to off-boarding) and not merely a separate stand-alone department tasked with 'creating diversity, inclusion, and belonging'.

In today's climate, some companies are starting to get much more explicit with their DI&B goals, which can look a lot like a quota. When looking at the measurable aspects of DI&B, often it is purely demographic data. Some argue that to actually move the needle in the numbers in material ways, they need to set some targets or goals for their teams. As a company, you have to determine where you are and where you would like to be from a pure representation perspective. Be careful because while this may be true, targets can often come across as quotas, which can lead to inauthentic DI&B programmes. The numbers are an important part, but just one part. Assessing diversity across a broader spectrum and considering inclusion and belonging is where the magic starts to happen from a company culture perspective.

> CULTURE QUOTE
>
> Listen to a lot of people (external experts, successful leaders) and then set up a facilitated, stakeholder-inclusive process that articulates how the defined culture will be exhibited, measured, valued, maintained, and updated.
>
> *Dr Sunita 'Sunny' Cooke, Superintendent/President at Mira Costa Community College District*

Walk the talk

Organizations who look at DI&B beyond a quota understand that true diversity starts at the top, with the leadership team and board of directors. Think about your leadership team. Literally picture them in your minds. How many men versus women are there? How many minorities are represented? What about your board of directors? Are they more diverse than your leadership team or do they look similar? How does that look compared to the demographics of the rest of your employee and customer base?

If your answers to the questions above showed a significant lack of diversity within your organization, sadly you are not alone. At the end of 2019, 26 of the S&P 500 and Fortune 1000 companies had achieved gender parity on their boards,[1] meaning the ratio of men to women was equal. That is not even 2.5 per cent, as there are 1,056 companies represented between them.

Some states, like California, have new regulations that require all public company boards have at least one female member by the end of 2021. Illinois and Georgia have passed similar legislation for boards, while no mandates exist with regards to a leadership team. Mandate or no mandate, there are real benefits to having diversity at the top. When you diversify leadership, you get a good representation of diverse perspectives, including those voices that are different from your own. Plus, studies, and our experience, have shown that organizations with greater diversity are more likely to outperform and have greater profits than organizations who are less diverse. While it is not accurate to say more diversity equals more profits, it is accurate to say organizations who take diversity, inclusion and belonging seriously are more likely to be successful. This happens for a few reasons.

First, remember what we said about CSR from the previous chapter and how it is used as a recruiting tool because employees want to be part of something bigger than themselves and do good for their local community? DI&B initiatives are similar. Employees want to work for organizations where they feel equally represented, understood, and not like an outsider. Remember when we said that things are more visible than you think and that people are watching and often making meaning of things? That applies here as well. We have seen top candidates turning down offers where they did not feel there was strong diversity represented in the leadership team or board of directors. Top talent is using this as a key indicator of an organization's culture when comparing competing job offers. Talent today wants to hear from different voices at the top. A survey conducted by Deloitte found that 72 per cent of the 1,300 employees surveyed would leave their organization for one that was more diverse, offering more DI&B initiatives and programmes.[2] Employees are serious about wanting different voices represented at the table and want to see the potential of growth to senior leadership for themselves.

A second reason organizations with more diversity are more successful is that people want to buy products and services from organizations who understand them. In fact, studies have shown that 70–80 per cent of all consumer purchase decisions are made by women.[3] As business leaders, offering products and services, this should greatly affect your marketing strategy. Having diverse perspectives at the top leads to better marketing, branding, and overall representation in the products and services you offer.

Achieving diversity on boards and on leadership teams is not about gender or race. It is about organizations accurately reflecting their employee base, their consumers, and their community and, in so doing, gaining a competitive advantage.

Measuring the ROI

One of the hardest parts about DI&B is measuring the return on investment, or ROI. Leaders often need a business case supported by quantification of the value of the programme before they begin implementation. While some organizations simply say they are making it a priority 'because it is the right thing to do', others are more convinced when you look through the ROI lens. Some DI&B initiatives are measured in feelings (how employees feel about their organization's DI&B programmes or the company overall). However, other initiatives can absolutely be measured in hard numbers. Remember, you can't manage what you don't measure. This is why it is important to understand your starting point first. After gathering feedback from all stakeholders, review the data.

> How employees feel about your organization's DI&B initiatives can be ascertained in a few ways. Engagement surveys can and should contain questions that help gauge how well your organization is doing to create a diverse and inclusive culture. However, you can also review Glassdoor, a website that allows current and former employees to rate their organizations anonymously. While the data on Glassdoor is self-reported, you can definitely see themes appearing. In fact, because Glassdoor is anonymous, employees may feel more open to write about their experiences. Another good source is employee exit interviews. One source of information that is often overlooked is your customers. If you want to know how your customers view your DI&B efforts, ask them. You can do customer surveys as well as review social media. Don't forget to review turnover data, promotion, and pay data (how often employees are getting promoted, which employees are being promoted or receiving pay increases, and how much they are receiving) and recruiting data around diversity of candidates in the pipeline. These are all sources of information that provide insights into where you are today.

As you review all the data, think about what areas within your business are doing well with regards to DI&B. What areas are lagging? It is not feasible, or realistic, to tackle all of the areas at once. Instead, use this data to narrow down which areas your organization should focus on and prioritize considering which ones will have the biggest impact. For example, if feedback from the engagement survey reveals that employees feel women are underrepresented in the engineering department, then this may become a focus area. Take a closer look at the data within your organization related to this. What percentage of the engineering department is female? When hiring for new roles, how many women are applying and being interviewed? Of those being interviewed, how many women are the final two candidates for the position? By answering these questions, you have a focused area and a starting point driven by hard numbers. You also have the metrics you will use to measure your progress in this area (percentage of females in the department, percentage of females being interviewed, etc). Next, set goals or put targets in place. Perhaps, in the example above, the goal is to achieve 50/50 gender parity by 2021. Be sure to set a time frame!

As you set these goals, be realistic. Consider all the options that might help you move the needle in achieving your goals. In the example above, if you want to increase the number of female candidates, are you building relationships with female universities and/or targeting a higher percentage of women in your internship programme? Being realistic with your goals will help as you engage hiring managers and other key stakeholders in the process. We are not saying don't shoot for the stars, but from our experience it takes multiple channels and firm commitment to see change happen.

When reviewing the engagement survey or other employee-reported feedback channels, keep perception and perspectives in mind. There may be a perception that there aren't many females in management in one department that happens to have very few female managers; the reality may be that the overall organization has more female managers than male managers. If reality is different than perception, you still have a problem. Think about how you communicate about diversity, inclusion and belonging in your organization. How transparent are you? Be sure you are clearly articulating where you do have diversity, where you still need to focus, and what you are asking people to do. Caution here, don't overcommit and under deliver. A strategy we've seen work well is a blended one that commits to actions in multiple areas, including inclusive leaders, inclusive teams, and initiatives that foster a sense of belonging and psychological safety.

It can be fairly straightforward to measure DI&B initiatives when they are as clear cut as the one mentioned with the number of female managers in a department. But what about DI&B training? How is this measured?

To see impact in DI&B training, we are looking to see measured results in employee behaviour, engagement, and team effectiveness. In working to raise the collective awareness of your organization in these areas, you can measure the actual number of trainings and number of people that participate. However, to see the real impact of these efforts, we want to see a raise in retention numbers, better scores on engagement surveys, and more voluntary participation in company events and activities.

An example of a significant effort related to raising the impact of inclusive leaders within an organization was one of our clients with over 80,000 employees globally that initiated an effort to train people managers from line managers to vice presidents on being Inclusion Champions. This was a significant investment of both time and money. This took the form of a full-day experiential class that helped people understand the reasons why DI&B is important, how it ties to their corporate values, and a very experiential learning experience where they both could increase their personal awareness and create a common language that would permeate the company culture. We helped deliver training to over 1,100 of their leaders in 2018. We could see personal changes in individuals at the end of a long day of training. It was common that people would walk in 'having to be there' and 'dreading another day of training', but what we found was that people left inspired. Inspired to work for an organization that was investing in them. Inspired to work for an organization that acknowledged them and all of their co-workers as individuals. Inspired to work for a company that united their large workforce with common values and a commitment to service standards. Finally, inspired to go back into the workplace and make a difference to individuals and their team overall. While the impact of this training may be difficult to measure in the short term, in the long term it should result in an increase in representation, a reduction in work conflict, higher engagement of these managers and their teams and an increase in collaboration across teams.

So, knowing how difficult it can be to measure certain areas of DI&B, why even bother? Because, just like in leadership and not addressing the elephant in the room, you can't bury your head in the sand and pretend you don't have an issue. We all have blind spots – things we don't see about ourselves but that others can see. Organizations can have these blind spots too. Identifying the metrics not only helps you determine which areas you have strengths in to leverage or areas you need to focus on, but also holds you accountable to identifying bias in your organizational blind spots. Below are some additional metrics that may be beneficial to review within your organization.

- *Representation*: This is just a general measure of each of the groups you want to monitor. You compare the percentages of employees in your company in those groups to the larger labour market as well as industry benchmarks. To make this even more meaningful, drill deeper by department. Keep in mind this metric doesn't take into account the levels or functions of the groups.
- *Retention*: Compare the average tenure for each of the monitored groups with the average tenure organization wide. You may notice a pattern of certain groups who are leaving the organization quicker than others. While the reasons for leaving could be varied (ie management, work, relocation), the data could point to some underlying issues with the culture.
- *Selection*: We already spoke about recruitment and ensuring you are interviewing a diverse slate of candidates. But take a closer look at the final candidates hired for each position. You are trying to see if there is a bias in the final selection made; a bias that may very well be a blind spot.
- *Training and development*: While we have already spoken about looking at your promotion numbers for the various groups, you also need to review your training and development numbers. Are there certain groups in your organization who are offered stretch assignments more than others? How about with leadership development programmes? Are only certain types of employee chosen for these opportunities?
- *Employer brand*: On your engagement survey, ask about your employer brand and how it resonates with employees. It may unintentionally favour or discriminate against certain types of employees over others. In turn, this will affect your recruitment efforts.

Employer brand and diversity

As we discussed in Chapter 6, the EVP is a key attraction and retention tool. It represents your culture, your identity, who you are. It helps you attract the right kind of talent you are looking for – the talent that will help you achieve your business priorities. But is it also working against you and turning certain high-performing candidates away?

First, and most obvious, are the colour schemes, images and graphics appealing to a wide range of candidates, to men and to women for example? When viewing your website, would a candidate with a family be just as interested in your organization as a candidate without a family? If you're unsure of how to answer these questions, start to hold focus groups or ask on the employee engagement survey how people feel about the EVP and branding. While surveys can (and should in most cases) remain anonymous, try to obtain demographics data such as gender, race, ethnicity, etc. Then, when asking questions, such as how employees feel about the employer brand, you can see whether it resonates with diverse populations.

Second, think about the language you are using. Does it convey inclusivity and authenticity or is it simply corporate jargon – common language and buzzwords to attract candidates? Interviewing your current employees and including quotes from them in your EVP goes a long way to build credibility. Tap into the diverse backgrounds at all levels to ensure everyone feels represented. Remember, you only have a few seconds to convey why top talent should work for you. What are your words really saying?

Take a look at your career site. Rather than having stock images, use photos of actual employees. Use these photos to help tell your story. Companies such as Lyft do just this on their careers page. They highlight their diversity and ask employees why they work for Lyft. It is personalized storytelling and ultimately the EVP is a story.

So you have diverse leadership, now what?

Achieving equal and fair representation is just the beginning. What do you plan to do with it? We have said countless times already that what leadership does is being watched and closely scrutinized by employees. In fact, employees are taking their cues from you. DI&B efforts are exactly the same, even once you've created a diverse leadership team.

A strong case of setting the right example at the top is TIAA's CEO, Roger Ferguson. In response to the racial injustice and the riots that followed the killing of George Floyd in the United States, Ferguson worked with his team to create a Be the Change programme. This programme comprised four pillars – facilitating change through understanding, dialogue, leadership, and action.[4] With this initiative, the organization created additional programmes and communications to articulate why this programme was created and what it was meant to do. Employees were encouraged to share personal stories and make commitments. They were asked to become active participants in helping TIAA remain diverse and to help eliminate systemic racism in their communities. There is power just in having the conversation and bringing it to the surface.

Employees want to know that you, as a leader, are committed to taking a stand and making a difference. They want to know that DI&B initiatives are personal to you. This can be very uncomfortable to some leaders. Have the leadership courage to lean into this vulnerability and your culture will benefit as well. Take a moment to develop your own leadership voice in this area and be able to articulate why diversity, inclusion and belonging are important to you and to your business.

Bringing it back to self-awareness

We started this book talking about how great cultures are built by leaders who do the work to develop their own sense of awareness. With regards to diversity, inclusion and belonging, this remains true. We all have perspectives and even biases. That isn't inherently bad. It's important to recognize that our perspectives are just that, and that others may offer experience and information that may shift or change our perspective. The willingness to listen and incorporate other perspectives into our own is a critical skill for leaders. We'd even challenge you to actively seek out other perspectives to learn; learn about your own bias, learn about others' experience.

One example of an invaluable learning experienced by a leader at the 80,000-employee client mentioned above was when she decided to start talking to her team about how they felt at work. In those conversations, she learned that for one colleague, when asked to complete the new hire paperwork and select a box representing his race, he was conflicted. He was raised by a single white mother, but his skin was not considered 'white'. Forced to make a selection, he selected 'African American' because he assumed that is what most people considered him to be. How eye-opening to look at the impact our processes, even government-mandated ones, may be having on our teams. In that conversation, the leader was able to learn about the employee's strong relationship with his mother and a lot more about the employee on a personal level. This deepened their relationship and her ability to connect with and inspire a member of her team.

We do not know what people go home to. For some, work might be the safest place they have. As leaders, we have an obligation to make the work environment not only one that fosters excellence, but one that encourages every member of our team to bring their best and know they will be seen and valued within the team. Reflect for a moment how well you know your team. It is not in everyone's nature to take the time to know their teams beyond the office walls. In today's world, understanding your team members as whole people will allow you to powerfully connect with them in authentic ways. The result is higher commitment, higher loyalty, and more personal motivation to bring their discretionary effort to your work.

Organizations are now recognizing that for leaders to be effective, they need to promote inclusiveness, belonging and holistic well-being. Regardless of your unique leadership style, these common competencies are now becoming table stakes for being effective leaders. To be a champion of your own culture, be willing to take a look at yourself, see where your learning edges are and be willing to dive in.

Common pitfalls

Diversity, inclusion, and belonging are areas where many organizations have not developed great comfort in how to infuse these efforts in a natural way into their regular business operations. While awareness has been increasing, there are still pitfalls to watch out for as you consider these concepts within your organization:

Avoidance. Get comfortable with the uncomfortable. The concepts of diversity, inclusion and belonging are not going away. It is likely that as the workforce continues to change, the burning platforms in these areas will too. That said, as leaders, we need to be willing to learn more about our own biases and create both personal and company perspectives in these areas. Picture an ostrich with its head in the sand here… do not do that.

Oversimplify. People are looking for action and leaders are feeling pressured to take it. This can result in taking some action that might 'check the box'. We cannot afford to believe that this absolves us of the responsibility to continue to gain understanding and infuse an intentional philosophy into our culture. The reference to diversity, inclusion, and belonging will evolve and continue to mean different things. Looking at our own biases, unconscious or otherwise, understanding the changing demographics in the workplace, and having honest reflection around the inclusiveness of our leaders and culture are now table stakes for business leaders to understand and incorporate into how they run their business.

Disregard feedback. All too often leaders want to disregard various forms of feedback. We talked about this related to employee surveys and it is certainly true of social feedback forums like Glassdoor. Resist the urge to explain away the feedback. Of course there is always the vengeful former employee with a lot to say, but often even in those comments, there are specks of truth. Look for trends, be honest and willing to consider what might be a root cause for some of the feedback and situations you are seeing.

Inauthenticity. We have all heard the reference to the 'token _____'. No one wants to be called the token of anything. It's rude and disrespectful. Hiring people just for their gender, race or other diverse characteristics is a shamefully transparent way to lack authenticity in DI&B efforts. Look for genuine ways to incorporate your understanding of why diversity, inclusion, and belonging are personally important to both you and your business so that your efforts are met with an authentic commitment to have a culture that values diversity and creates an environment conducive for all members to contribute their best.

Questions to ask

DI&B initiatives remain at the top of the list for HR. However, just like culture, these initiatives are not just the job of HR. All employees,

---

QUESTIONS TO ASK – ASSESSING DIVERSITY, INCLUSION, AND BELONGING

- How diverse is our board of directors?
- How diverse is our leadership team?
- What have we done to create awareness of unconscious bias in our organization?
- Is there a significant difference between the diversity represented in our overall employee population compared to that of our management team?
- Have we taught our leaders what it means to be inclusive leaders? Are they implementing that learning?
- Have we incorporated any questions around DI&B into our engagement survey or other employee feedback mechanisms?
- How transparent are we in regard to both our DI&B metrics (data) and initiatives in these areas?
- Have we engaged the employee population to be part of the solution? How?
- Have we evaluated the link between our DI&B efforts and our corporate social responsibility initiatives? How can these be more connected?
- What role am I playing in the perception of DI&B in our workplace?

especially the leadership team, need to take an active role. The box below provides some questions that will help you as you look for starting points or in creating a potential roadmap on your diversity, inclusion and belonging journey.

Moving to action: what you can do next

DI&B initiatives continue to be at the forefront of employees' minds when they are considering staying with your organization or finding a new opportunity. Here are some things you can do to bring DI&B to life within your organization:

Consider non-traditional talent sources. Oftentimes, when organizations post open requisitions for new jobs, they are thinking about people who are 'working age'. While this is defined as age 15-64, age 23-55 is a more realistic target. However, this eliminates a wide swath of people who could contribute greatly to your organization. Some non-traditional talent sources include interns and early career hires, return-to-work hires (parents rejoining the workforce), elderly workers, and even company alumni who may have entered the gig economy. While you may have some very specific requirements depending on the position, we would suggest thinking about tasks and projects that these non-traditional talent sources may excel at. Consider how you draft the job description. Do you really require 15–20 years of experience and someone who has been there, done that for this specific role? Does that limit the pool of potential candidates for your role? Perhaps someone who is agile, has demonstrated the ability to learn, grow, and be resourceful can solve new problems and represent different segments of your customer and partner demographic instead. Today's workforce is adapting at an unprecedented pace; what opportunities do these changes provide to your organization? How flexible are you in work hours, in location, in scope of work?

Embed diversity into the recruiting process. Ensuring you have a diverse workforce and culture starts with interviewing diverse candidates. If you think back to the definitions we stated at the beginning of this chapter, we do not mean diversity just in terms of skin colour or ethnicity. Interview candidates with varying degrees and levels of experience. Keep an open mind as to the type of background that you think would be a good 'fit' for your organization. In addition, be sure that you assemble a diverse interview panel. It is easy to forget that candidates are interviewing you just as much as you are interviewing them. In that initial face-to-face interview, candidates are basing their opinions on what they see first. Then they are seeing how this view aligns with your organization's action. If the two do not align, chances are the candidate may not want to work for you. For example, if you state that women in leadership is important to your organization, yet only 2 per cent of leaders are women, there is a misalignment. Best practices in this area ensure that final candidate slates for open positions include a targeted amount of diversity. Of course, you will select the best candidate, but if you do not have any diversity in the candidates you are considering, you for sure will not end up hiring a diverse set of employees.

Create Employee Resource Groups (ERGs). ERGs are self-managed groups within organizations formed by employees with shared characteristics or experiences. By allowing employees to form their own subcommunities and share their experiences, they can support each other and gain exposure to employees at various levels throughout the organization. ERGs can include groups such as veterans, African Americans, women in the workplace, working parents, etc. One word of caution when employees want to create ERGs: be sure they are not perpetuating feelings of isolationism. For example, men should be invited to the women's ERG meeting. This allows for a richer dialogue and the ability to establish a shared understanding of one another.

Conduct a bias audit. Consider conducting an audit to look at all of your standard practices through the lens of finding bias. Bias comes in all kinds: unconscious bias, confirmation bias, halo effect, horn effect, 'like me' bias, selection bias, status quo bias and more. Forward-looking organizations are looking for ways to eliminate unintended bias from their organizations and one way to do that is to start with an audit and see what you might not be aware of.

Lessons from the real world

Why do you think diversity, inclusion and belonging is important to a company culture, company performance and success?

> Unless everyone in any culture, especially company culture, truly feels valued and respected there will always be an undercurrent of discomfort that will eventually manifest in one of several ways: volatile interactions, uncertainty about whether to speak up, and ambiguity about one's worth in the eyes of others when one does find the courage to speak up. Company performance and success are dependent upon every voice being valued.
>
> *Dr Anita Polite-Wilson, Founder and CEO at Dr Anita Enterprises, Inc*

> DI&B generate the creativity, resources, access/permission, energy, and collaboration that enable individuals, companies, and humanity to move towards their fullest potential. One way DI&B creates this effect is through providing information. This information can come from within ourselves (by including more of one's under-tapped skills, identities, styles of thought, etc), as well as unique needs/perspectives of others that improve our results. Taken together, this information generates new ideas, a more holistic mindset, and results that better speak to a wide variety of customers. I believe DI&B has surfaced from the need to heal traumas within individual psyches that result from and proliferate life-negating patterns and experiences. Thus, DI&B promotes the thriving of people, work, and planet.
>
> *Rona Kremer, Diversity, and Inclusion Program Manager at Dolby Laboratories*

What advice do you have to a leader who wants to create a more inclusive culture in their organization?

> Exercise the intellectual humility to get educated on the purpose of DI&B and really understand it. For example, the term White Privilege makes most people – not just white people – uncomfortable. When the term is

understood, it actually opens possibilities for white privilege to serve a purpose by using that privilege to intentionally make space for all people of colour. Using one's individual power to share one's power and in turn empower others creates powerful teams. That is part of the purpose of DI&B.

Dr Anita Polite-Wilson, Founder and CEO at Dr Anita Enterprises, Inc

Begin by learning what inclusion is and how it impacts people at work. If you need a starting point, use self-awareness. What parts of yourself do you not include at work and what impact does that have on you, your work, and your team? What makes you feel excluded or included? To create a more inclusive culture in your organization, you might look at the results of employee surveys (or solicit feedback from your own team). Pick one dynamic of exclusion, and help your team co-create and implement a proactive behaviour of inclusion, along with an agreement of accountability for that behaviour. Get ongoing feedback and keep iterating – if you can experience the fun and rewarding nature of this work, that could help others feel the same way and want to help.

Rona Kremer, Diversity, and Inclusion Programme Manager at Dolby Laboratories

The number one thing I would say is for leaders to ask more questions. Be curious about your people. In order to be inclusive, we need to understand our people... what drives them, what frustrates them, and what is important to them.

Tacy Riehm, Founder, Leadership Consultant, Speaker and Executive Coach at Vos Consulting, LLC

Final thoughts

Diversity, inclusion and belonging is a very personal topic for many. We constantly talk about bringing our authentic selves to work or listening and learning from diverse perspectives. But how often are we actually doing these things in our organizations? From a Total Rewards well-being perspective, the ability to feel safe at work in order to be ourselves is hugely important. As leaders, these uncomfortable topics should not and cannot be avoided if you want to create an exceptional organizational culture.

Take a few minutes to write down two to three key takeaways from this chapter with regards to your organization's DI&B efforts. Do you have any DI&B initiatives? If so, have they been effective? Do you know how to measure your DI&B initiatives? What role have you played and what role do you need to play with regards to these efforts? How does it connect to your culture work? Now, review what you wrote and next to each takeaway write down one action item that you will commit to doing to ensure your organization creates a strong DI&B strategy in alignment with the culture you are working to create.

What have you committed to do?

Endnotes

1 Sahadi, J (2019) More women are on big company boards, but the numbers are still shockingly low, *CNN*, 15 November, https://www.cnn.com/2019/11/15/success/women-board-members-gender-gap/index.html (archived at https://perma.cc/NG6Q-JLMB)

2 Deloitte (2017) Inclusion Pulse Survey, https://www2.deloitte.com/content/dam/Deloitte/us/Documents/about-deloitte/us-about-deloitte-inclusion-survey.pdf (archived at https://perma.cc/XAZ8-HFUB)

3 Brennan, B (2015) Top 10 things everyone should know about women consumers, *Forbes*, 21 January, https://www.forbes.com/sites/bridgetbrennan/2015/01/21/top-10-things-everyone-should-know-about-women-consumers/#94f12e6a8b44 (archived at https://perma.cc/U42P-TQWP)

4 Estrada, S (2020) How TIAA's diverse leadership aims to support racial justice from the top down, *HR Dive*, 06 July, https://www.hrdive.com/news/how-tiaas-diverse-leadership-aims-to-support-racial-justice-from-the-top-d/581049/ (archived at https://perma.cc/79HE-4WRV)

10

Moving to action

Organizational culture has the biggest impact on two things critical to business valuation and brand – the ability to make and keep commitments (credibility) and the ability to drive and deliver results (execution).

IAN ZISKIN, PRESIDENT OF EXEC EXCEL GROUP LLC

If you have made it this far, you have learned about organizational culture, organizational structure, core values, attracting and retaining the right talent, engagement, motivation, rewards, diversity, inclusion, and belonging…

Exhausted yet?

As you can tell, creating an exceptional organizational culture is a lot of work but totally worth it! You are clearly serious about wanting to ensure your company succeeds into the future and that you design a company culture that will enable it. We know it has been a lot of information to take in and really think about. Changes do not happen overnight.

The trick is not in understanding the information; it is in making it stick and bringing others along.

Rather than leave you with only information, we are going to show you how to actually put this plan into action.

We started out by identifying the three lenses that are important when thinking about organizational culture: yourself as a leader, your team as an example, and the organization as a whole. We use the word *culture* so frequently, but how often do we pause to really think about what it means? What does it look like? What does it feel like? It's an intangible concept, yet like a sixth sense, we know when it's not good.

Next, we explored the intentionality of culture and why top-performing cultures don't happen by accident. We took a closer look at your role as a leader and the importance of individual development and self-awareness in shaping organizational culture. Do you remember your thoughts about your own leadership style when you read the traits of a self-aware leader in Chapter 2? How are you feeling with regards to your own self-awareness and your role in building a truly magical culture? Perhaps you have some ideas about how you might gain more self-awareness or improve on known development areas. We also discussed how critical it is to make culture a part of the regular organizational discussion.

After looking at the importance of leaders developing their own self-awareness, we began to walk through the various components of building an exceptional organizational culture, starting with organizational structure. We talked about the close tie between the culture you want to create and the structure you have in place. Do you have a structure in place that will help drive the culture you want or is it a potential barrier? As you began to consider thinking about teams differently and being open to looking for talent in non-traditional ways, we got clear about defining leadership expectations and the role of the leader in finding great talent. Finally, we emphasized the need to have a great HR team to help you define and build the right team.

After the discussion on structure and looking at designing your teams, we moved into the need to define core values in creating a sustainable culture and the importance of connecting HR programmes and policies to these core values. Think about your organization. Are there areas where your core values are not fully integrated and should be? Are there leaders whose behaviours are not aligned with the values as well? If the answer to either of these questions is *yes*, what are you willing to do about it? When? Now?

Continuing down the path of building an exceptional culture, we started to look at defining core competencies or skills needed in your employees to build a truly exceptional and aligned culture and the roles of these skills, along with Total Rewards, in attracting, retaining, engaging, and motivating employees. Finally, we ended with an eye on diversity, inclusion and belonging and the critical role they play in creating a culture where all employees are able to and want to bring their discretionary effort every day.

As we mentioned at the beginning, this is not the type of book that you read once, put on your bookshelf, and never open again. We hope the pages are written in, highlighted, and earmarked for you to come back to time and time again. This is a journey and it does not have a straightforward path. If you have made it this far, we know you are serious about wanting a truly long-lasting and high-performing culture.

While development is continuous, organizations are also dynamic, as is the world in which they operate. What this translates to is developing the ability to ebb and flow and create an infrastructure, systems, and processes to remain agile.

Throughout this book, you have had realizations and identified some clear actions that would help you evolve your organizational culture. At the end of each chapter we asked you to write down some key takeaways and actionable steps that you commit to taking to ensure you are designing an exceptional organizational culture. Make sure that list is near you for this chapter.

So how do we make these changes long-lasting?

Here's how.

Remember all those 'Moving to action: what you can do next' sections at the end of each chapter? Now we are going to weave them together to create an action plan you can revisit time and time again. It is a quick checklist to make sure you are organized and building and maintaining the kind of culture you are really after. Come back to these questions at least every year, if not every six months, to see if you are still on the right path. Building an exceptional organizational culture takes time, effort, energy, and pivots. No one expected the COVID-19 pandemic to shift the way we work, yet here we are. These crises also shape our culture and require leaders to shift priorities. As you go through the exercise below, keep crisis management, your organizational strategy, and your individual leadership traits in mind.

Organizational culture

1 In no more than three sentences, briefly describe your organizational culture today.
2 In no more than three sentences, briefly describe the organizational culture you would like to see.
3 Perform a gap analysis between your answer to the first question and your answer to the second question. What areas should you prioritize your focus on in order to achieve the culture you would like to see?

Organizational structure

1 Write down two elements of your current organizational structure that are working well and two elements that may not be serving your culture.
2 Why do these elements work/not work with your culture?
3 For the two elements that could use a little work (or maybe you've identified more), write down two actionable steps you will take to turn them into elements that work for your culture rather than against your culture.

Core values

1 On a scale of 1–10, with 1 being *Not at All* and 10 being *Extremely Well*, how well do your current core values serve your organization and culture?
2 Why did you give your core values the rating that you did?
3 Write down two to three areas in your organization where you see the core values misrepresented or not represented at all.

4 For these areas, write down two actionable steps you will take to ensure the values are accurately represented.

Key competencies

1 What changes in the business and operating environment have occurred that have affected the types of skills and competencies that are required from employees?
2 Which of your current skills and competencies do you need to adjust to based on the change in business conditions?
3 If your organization has key competencies defined, review how they are communicated to employees and used in various programmes, such as the performance management process. Write down two to three actionable steps you can take to ensure your employees are aware of their expectations and key competencies of the organization.
4 If your organization does not have key competencies defined, write down two to three actionable steps you will take to help your organization, or even your team, start this process.

Attracting and retaining talent

1 Write down two to three attributes that make your organization unique.
2 Write down your organization's Employee Value Proposition (EVP). If your organization does not have a formal EVP, write down what you think the EVP is.
3 Ask two to three other leaders in your organization what they believe the company EVP is. Write their responses below.
4 If there is a gap between what you think it is and what they think it is, why do you think that gap exists?
5 Keeping this EVP in mind, write down two to three ways you can start incorporating this EVP into your hiring and interviewing practices and/or communication practices when hiring talent.

Engaging and motivating talent

1 Review the most recent employee survey results. Look at the top two to three areas and the bottom two to three areas. In your opinion, write down why you feel employees rated these items the way they did.
2 Write down two to three actionable steps that you can take to help move the bottom two to three up.
3 Generally, we can glean a lot of information from the types of issues we routinely see arise in an organization. What are the top two to three issues you have seen? These could be behavioural, training, etc.
4 What will you commit to doing to address those issues?

Total Rewards

1 Write down the top three to four benefits/perks that employees value the most.
2 How do you know they value these the most?
3 Do these same benefits/perks align with stakeholders at all levels of the organization? If yes, how so and if no, why not?
4 How do these benefits/perks align with the culture you would like to see? Write down two to three actionable steps you can take to ensure what is important to employees is also aligned with your culture.

Diversity, inclusion, and belonging

1 Take a close look at your organization. Think about the board of directors, the executive team, the broader management team, and the employee base as a whole. Do you feel there are diverse backgrounds represented and included in important discussions? Why do you feel the way that you do?

2 Write down three to four actionable steps you can take immediately, whether at the organizational level or within your own team, to help all employees feel more included, accepted, and authentic.

Remember: action plans only work if you *act*. Instead of doing things the way you have always done them (because it is easier, more cost-effective, or comfortable), resist the urge to stay stagnant. Push past your own self-imposed limitations to create something better – for your employees and yourself.

The importance of change management

Culture change is perhaps one of the biggest transformation initiatives that organizations undergo. Even if you aren't overhauling your entire culture at one time, which we do not recommend by the way, you will need to harness the strong elements of your culture to help you transform others.

So why doesn't change last? There are many reasons for this. First, employees may be sceptical due to failed change efforts in the past. Much like the engagement survey, if you've committed to change, you need to follow it through and make it successful. A second reason could be that employees do not feel invested in the change process. Remember, you need employees if you want to have a strong organizational culture and a successful business for that matter. Employee buy-in is key to ensuring changes actually stick. Another reason change fails is because employees simply do not understand the reason for the change. Enrol all employees in the change process. Start with the why – why are we making this change? Clearly articulate what problem you are solving. Consider what other competing priorities you may have going on in the organization which could cause change fatigue and actually frustrate employees more. Lastly, changes do not last because the systems, processes and potentially the incentives do not support the change. Culture change cannot be a half-baked idea. You need to think through all areas of the change and all potential places that could be impacted (ie policies, performance management, etc).

With so many reasons that change doesn't work, how can you create sustainable, long-lasting change? First, you can believe in the changes you are making. Don't make changes to keep up with your competitors or in reaction to a few employees leaving. Truly think about why the change is important and then stand behind it 100 per cent. Second, don't boil the ocean. Focus on a few areas at a time, starting with the most critical. We would suggest starting with core values if you don't already have them. Finally, expand change capabilities to all levels within the organization, not just leadership, and ensure there is communication alignment. This is where change management principles can help.

Whatever actions you decide to take, it is important to remember the fundamentals about change management. An effective change management strategy will make or break any culture transformation initiatives you undergo. Change management is about how you prepare and support employees to successfully adapt to the change in order to drive the desired outcomes and overall organizational success. From slight changes to holistic business transformation, you want to bring people along with you on that journey.

There are many change management models available for you to tap into. Depending on the level and impact of the changes you are making, one model may be better for you than another. Below are a few types of change management models to get you thinking about which may be best in your situation:

- **Lewin's Change Management Model.** This is a three-step process whereby you first unfreeze your current processes and policies to review how things are done today. You then make the necessary changes before refreezing.
- **The McKinsey 7-S Model.** As the name suggests, this model consists of seven S's (strategy, structure, systems, shared values, style, staff, and skills). You answer a series of questions about each of the seven areas and then you cross-examine each area to find out what changes you actually need to implement.
- **Kotter's 8 Steps to Change Management.** This model focuses more on the people behind the changes than on the actual changes themselves. This model focuses on a sense of urgency, buy-in,

removing barriers and setting the changes. We use this model often because of its focus on people. See the breakout box below for more information on this model.
- **The ADKAR Model.** Similar to Kotter's model, the ADKAR model focuses on the particular individuals behind the change. Unlike Kotter's model, this is a bottom-up method focused more on a set of goals to reach around awareness, desire, knowledge, ability and reinforcement (hence the name, ADKAR).
- **Bridges' Transition Model.** This model taps into the semantics and emotions behind the word *change*. In place of *change* the word *transition* is used because transition is more of a journey rather than a perceived abrupt change or shift. This model guides employees through letting go of what was and entering a new beginning, with a neutral zone in the middle to serve as a bridge.

What we've outlined are just five of the many change management models available. Our goal isn't to tell you which one is best; it's simply to say that change is hard and using a change management model can assist in creating sustainable and long-lasting change.

KOTTER'S 8-STEP APPROACH TO CHANGE MANAGEMENT

We like to reference the theory developed by John Kotter in his 8-Step Approach to Change Management when looking at any kind of organizational change. Here are the basics of the important steps to consider as you embark on any change efforts:

Increase Urgency: Ensure that you build the case for change. Look for ways to get both rational and emotional buy-in from all stakeholders. Ensure that you have clarified leadership involvement, roles, and expectations. Be sure to identify all potential stakeholders and change impacts, build buy-in with leaders and impacted groups alike.

Build Guiding Teams: Determine the right approach for the project or initiative. Engage the right people, set clear team goals, create a climate of trust and commitment. Involving people in the change will help get a positive outcome.

> *Get the Vision Right*: Create a compelling, motivating picture of the future to enrol people in the desired future state. This is important; we started this book with identifying your why. People need to understand not only where you want to go, but why and why now.
>
> *Communicate for Buy-In*: Ensure continuous multi-directional dialogue and feedback. Continue to ensure stakeholder enrolment in the change. Keep all stakeholders informed of implementation plans, how they are impacted, and what changes they can expect and when.
>
> *Enable Action*: Identify early adopters and potential resistors. Confront resistance and be willing to work through barriers. Allocate the appropriate resources, training and materials to ensure people have the tools for success.
>
> *Look for Low-Hanging Fruit*: Create quick wins in the initial phases of change. Acknowledge and recognize these quick wins in a public way. Reward the right behaviours.
>
> *Persist*: Do not let up and leverage the momentum of your great start. Ensure your message is not just the flavour of the month.
>
> *Sustain*: Make it stick, keep the messaging going, weave it into your regular communications cadence. Monitor progress, identify ways to assess the impact of the change and the alignment towards the initial vision and business results.

Final thoughts

Curating a truly exceptional culture isn't a checklist item. It takes time, commitment, passion, and a desire to do what is right, both for the organization and for the employees. Culture isn't owned by any one individual and it certainly isn't something HR controls. There is no magic wand for creating a good culture. What we've described to you in these pages is a journey that defines your leadership legacy. Now is the time to look at your organization, your culture, your employees, and the values you stand for.

Are you doing everything you can to be inclusive?

Are you fostering the best culture?

Are you showing up as the most effective leader you can?

Are you open to change and feedback?

Be an active participant in your own growth and development. The future of your work – and world – depends on it.

You've got this.

INDEX

accidental core values 76
accountability 18, 21, 25, 105, 192
   and engagement/motivation 148, 160, 161, 162
   organizational structure 53, 54, 55, 73
acquisitions 87, 114
action plans 217–21
actions 11–12, 31–32, 36
ad hoc incentive plans 187
adaptability 53, 63, 102, 111, 115, 120, 121
ADKAR Model 223
Adobe 84
agile teams 52, 53
agility 52, 53, 63, 102–03, 111, 112, 120, 179, 209, 217
Airbnb 84
alienation 34
all-employee (town hall) meetings 79, 80, 85, 108, 158
Amazon 136
anticipating change 108–09
aspirational core values 76
audits 37, 97, 210
authenticity 21, 44, 95, 97, 105, 128, 206, 212
   see also inauthenticity
autonomy 69, 121, 130, 160
avoidance 38, 207

Baby Boomers 184
bad leadership 30–31
bad management 31, 38
balcony perspective 34, 47
base pay (salary) 172, 175, 176, 183, 191
Be the Change programme 205
behaviour tests 37
behavioural-based interviews 138–39
behavioural competencies 112
behavioural values 83
behaviours 11–12, 31, 35–36, 41–42, 43, 77, 86
   see also behaviour tests; behavioural-based interviews; behavioural competencies; behavioural values
belief 82, 83
belief lid 82
beliefs 6, 12, 33–34, 35, 103
   see also values

belonging 19, 24, 57–58, 84, 103, 195–213, 220–21
belonging assessment 208, 220–21
benefits package 173, 178–79, 180–81, 191
   medical 182, 187, 189
   see also perks
bereavement leave 180–81
bias 103, 137, 202, 203, 205, 207, 210
bias audits 210
biotech sector 111, 177
blame culture 38, 56
bonding questions 48–49
bonuses (incentive plans) 89, 135–36, 163, 172, 174, 178, 183, 187, 188, 191
brainstorming 76, 106
brand
   customer 17, 127–28
   employer 17, 92, 94, 118, 132–33, 135, 145, 203–04
   leadership 13–14
Bridges' Transition Model 223
bureaucratic culture 38, 142
burnout 67–68
business process teams 52, 53
business strategy 27, 57, 68, 71, 112, 114, 117, 182–83, 188
   see also objectives
buy-in 9, 86, 163, 221, 223, 224

California 198
call centres 72, 116
Canva 128, 132
career development (growth) 55, 57, 60, 71, 72, 130, 148, 173–74, 175, 203
   see also career-pathing; promotions
career-pathing 53, 62, 71
career sites 204
cash (money) 148–49, 172–73, 191
challenge 42, 120, 130, 162–63
change 102, 108–09, 134, 152
change management 18–20, 48, 87, 133, 221–24
Chief Strategy Officers 183
coaching 5–6, 25, 47, 120, 161, 173
collaboration 24, 28, 53, 76, 105, 112, 119, 202, 211

college education (degrees) 58–59, 141
commitment 152, 157, 158, 201, 206
common core values 76
communication 19, 32, 35–37, 88, 105, 106–07, 224
    and engagement 151, 152–53, 156, 164–65
    rewards programmes 188
    talent sourcing 132–33
    see also connection (interaction); dialogue; difficult conversations; feedback; focus groups; language; listening; message construction
compensation 89, 152, 171, 172–73, 178, 190
    see also base pay (salary); bonuses (incentive plans); cash (money)
competencies 101–23, 159, 219
competencies assessment 219
competency customization 111–12
competency requirement reviews 114
complacency 42, 184
connection (interaction) 21, 31, 79, 121, 148, 154–58
consistency 14, 31, 53, 81, 105, 113, 133, 148
consultants 56, 62, 69, 72, 157, 168, 178
contradictory values 95
control 38, 43, 55, 69, 72
coordination 55
core competencies 102–09, 112, 113–14, 122–23
core values 17–18, 31, 36, 65, 75–100, 174–75, 180–82, 222
core values assessment 78, 96–97, 218–19
core values data collection 79–82
core values definition process 78–86
core values group exercise 80
core values survey 80–82
core values team 78–79, 80, 82, 88, 129
corporate social responsibility (CSR) 184–86, 208
COVID-19 63, 107, 114, 119, 121, 173, 185–86
creativity 62, 63, 84, 106, 121, 144, 167, 175
crisis management 107–08, 109
critical thinking 103, 115
cross-functional working 52, 54, 111, 133, 166, 183, 190
cultural intelligence 103–04, 114
culture, defined 11–12, 137
Culture Ambassador programme 92
culture assessment 22–24, 28–29, 46, 155

culture change 43, 48, 221–22
culture committees 138, 178
culture fit 92, 137
culture stickiness 44–45
curiosity 84, 212
customer-based structures 52, 53
customer brand 17, 127–28
customer focus 104, 113–14
customer service 18, 95, 116, 132, 136
    see also guest experience
customer surveys 200
customer value proposition 127–28
customization 53, 111–12, 141, 154

data collection (gathering) 79–82, 107, 200
decision making 14, 17, 40, 54, 64–65, 69, 85, 88–89, 155
demographics 184, 197, 204, 207, 209
design thinking 105–06, 151
development *see* career development; leadership development (management development)
DI&B *see* belonging; diversity; inclusion
dialogue 16, 24, 29, 46, 79, 205, 224
differentiation 55, 97, 162, 191
difficult conversations 37, 121
digital proficiency 119
disengagement 39
diversity 57–58, 95, 103, 137–38, 195–213
diversity assessment 208, 220–21
diversity data 200

early adopters 224
EEO-1 196–97
8 Steps to Change Management 223–24
emotional intelligence 34, 48, 103, 114, 158
    see also self-awareness
emotions 32, 34, 49, 103
employee recognition 31, 91, 172, 174, 175, 177, 184, 187, 190, 191
employee resource groups 76, 210
employee value proposition *see* EVP
employees 5, 12, 29–30, 60, 63
    and core values 79–82
    full-time 61, 63, 66, 126
    see also benefits package; buy-in; employee recognition; employee resource groups; engagement; EVP; exit interviews; female workers
employer brand 17, 92, 94, 118, 132–33, 135, 145, 203–04
empowerment 6, 13, 18, 53, 85, 147, 158, 160, 212

end-user needs 106
engagement 60, 61, 147–69, 177, 204, 220
    see also disengagement
engagement assessment 166, 220
engagement survey completion rate 153
engagement survey length 151–52
engagement survey timing 152
engagement surveys 149–53, 164, 166–67, 200, 204, 220
entrepreneurial mindset 91, 106
environmental strategies 184, 185
Equal Employment Opportunity Commission 196
Equal Employment Opportunity survey 196–97
equity (fairness) 181–82
equity (ownership) 172, 175
ERGs 76, 210
EVP 127–35, 140, 142–44, 145–46, 204, 219–20
EVP assessment 130–31, 143
EVP reviews 133–34
EVP statements (sentences) 132, 145
EVP teams 129–30, 131
execution 107, 111, 116
executive team 6, 78, 93, 129–30, 131, 140, 143, 144, 157–58
exit interviews 41, 200
Expedia 29
experiences rewards 177
expert teams 60, 62, 164
experts 187, 197
external leadership development 110–11
external lens (outside perspective) 98, 157
External Mobility 98
external survey providers 166–67

Facebook 145, 181
feedback 29–30, 46, 86, 148, 151, 154–58, 168, 178, 207, 212
    see also engagement surveys; listening
feedback loops 29–30
female workers 198, 200–01
Ferguson, Roger 205
filters 35
fixed pay 172, 175, 183
flexibility 53, 115, 119, 121, 130, 145, 173, 191, 192, 209
flow state (state of flow) 163, 167, 168
focus groups 79–80, 85, 92, 106, 108, 130, 158, 166, 204
formal structures 64
founders, and values 94–95
Four Seasons Hotel 85

4th Industrial Revolution 104
freelancers 60
full-time employees 60, 61, 63, 66, 126
fun 44
functional structures 52, 53, 54
future-focused questions 28, 109

gap analysis 131–32, 218
gender parity 198, 200
    see also female workers
general core values 76
genetic leaders 109–10
geographical structures 52, 53, 55
Georgia 198
gift cards 91, 176, 177
gig economy (workers) 60, 61–63, 67, 69, 157, 209
Glassdoor 41, 143, 200, 207
goals 32, 57, 197, 201
    see also objectives
Golden Circle, The 77
Golden Rule 85
good leaders 31–32
Google 145, 180
Gravity Payments 107–08
grief leave 181
group exercise, core values 80
guest experience 85
    see also customer service
guiding teams 224

hackathons 167
health insurance 191
hierarchical structures 54
high performance 4–5, 9, 126
higher education 58
    see also college education (degrees)
hiring see talent sourcing (hiring)
honesty 59, 76, 81, 87, 168
HR function 41, 66, 72–73, 74, 78, 114, 130, 131, 152–53, 154
HubSpot 132
hybrid structures 52, 53
hypothetical questions 144

ideas generation 134
Illinois 198
inauthenticity 197, 207–08
    see also authenticity
incentive bonuses 89, 135–36, 163, 172, 174, 178, 183, 187, 188, 191
inclusion 57–58, 76, 85, 103, 182, 195–213
inclusion assessment 208, 220–21
inclusion champions 202

individualization 135
influencing skills 83, 108, 121
informal discussions 154–58
informal structures 64
information sharing 24, 65, 120, 165
innovation 53, 63, 81, 84, 85, 87, 112, 121, 154
intangible rewards 183
integration 55
intellectual humility 211–12
intent versus impact 35–36, 94
internal candidates 141
interview panels 210
interview questions 144
interviews 138–39, 142, 144, 209–10
  see also exit interviews
iterative approach 121, 212

job competencies 114
job descriptions 57–59, 78, 142, 162, 209
job features 145
job necessities 145
job opportunities 145
job quality 145

Kotter's 8 Steps to Change Management 223–24

labour practices 185
language 35, 118, 142, 202, 204
leadership 12–14, 21–24, 29–40, 64–65, 83, 109–10, 116, 143, 155, 161
  competencies for 113, 122
  and core values 77–78, 92–94, 98
  and DI&B 198–99
  recruiting (planning for) 140
  see also executive team; leadership development (management development); servant leadership
leadership development (management development) 110–11, 112, 119, 203
leadership effectiveness assessment 13–14, 155
leadership pitfalls 21
leadership recruitment 116, 140
leadership role definition 116
leadership values 13–14, 83
learning 24, 110, 121
leave policies 180–82
leaving organizations (separation) 119, 131, 148–49, 199, 203
  see also exit interviews
leveraged resources 55
Lewin's Change Management Model 222

Likert scale 131
lines of business structures 52, 53, 55
listening 23–24, 105, 134, 158–59, 205
long-term focus 19, 47, 68–69, 111
low-hanging fruit 23, 74, 224
low performers 67, 161, 167
loyalty 148, 149, 153, 154, 206
Lyft 204

management attention 55
management behaviour 31, 38, 148, 156–57
  see also micromanagement
management development (leadership development) 110–11, 112, 119, 203
marginalized leaders 65
Marketing function 54, 68–69, 80, 88, 129, 133, 199
Mastercard 181
matrix performance evaluation 89–90
matrix structures 52, 53, 54
McKinsey 7-S Model 222–23
meaningful work 3, 60, 173
measurement (metrics) 24, 48, 159, 161, 163–64, 199–203
medical benefits 179, 180, 182, 187, 189
mergers 87, 114
message construction 35, 133, 224
micromanagement 160
Millennials 184
minor organizational tensions 71
mission 75, 77
  see also purpose
money (cash) 148–49, 172–73, 191
motivation 31, 40, 55, 60, 147–69, 176–77, 220
motivation assessment 166, 220
'must haves' skills 59
MVV see mission; values; vision

negatives focus 43
negotiation 108
new hire onboarding (orientation) 91–92, 118–19, 136, 156
'niceness' culture 148, 165
non-self-aware leaders 38–40
non-traditional talents sources 209

objectives 32, 130, 183
  see also business strategy; goals
Offer, The 136
onboarding (orientation) 91–92, 118–19, 136, 156
one-on-one meetings 46, 98, 158, 173
operational values 83

opt out bonuses 135–36
organizational culture assessment 218
organizational layers (levels) 54, 70, 72, 110
organizational network analysis tools 64
organizational restructuring 67–68, 69–70
organizational structure 51–74, 88, 103, 110, 218
organizational structure assessment 52, 67, 218
organizational tensions 16–17, 42, 46, 65, 69, 71–72, 95
organizational values 11–12, 29, 41, 97–98, 137, 178
    see also core values
outside perspective (external lens) 98, 157
oversimplification 207
ownership 25, 77, 81, 105

pay data 200
pay mix 183–84
    see also base pay (salary); fixed pay; money (cash); variable pay
Pay to Quit 136
peer recognition programmes 91, 191
performance disconnect 161
performance evaluation (reviews) 24, 89–90, 113–14, 161–62, 167
performance 161, 167
    see also low performers; performance evaluation (reviews); underperformance
perks 62, 128, 132, 164, 171, 175, 190, 192, 220
permanent employees 63
persistence 224
personal connection (interaction) 21, 31, 79, 121, 148, 154–58
personal questions 156
personal strengths 32, 33, 115
personal weaknesses 32, 33, 34
personalization 85, 88, 176–80
philanthropic strategies 185, 186
points-based rewards systems 177
policies 88, 132, 159, 180–82, 185–86
positional power 21
positive accidental core values 76
positive culture 28, 44, 191
positives focus 43
previous rewards programmes 187–88
processes 17, 54, 73–74, 105–06, 121, 162, 206, 217, 221, 222
product-based structures 52, 53, 55
productivity 39, 102, 126

project definition (redefinition) 59–61
project management (managers) 60, 104
promotions 89, 110, 116, 119, 141, 159, 162, 183, 200
purpose 3, 4, 9, 31, 134
    see also mission

RACI charts 73
recognition 31, 91, 172, 174, 175, 177, 184, 187, 190, 191
recruitment 118, 198–99, 209–10
    see also gig economy (workers); interviews; talent sourcing (hiring)
recruitment misalignment 210
Regulatory function 55
remote working 7, 19, 61, 97, 105, 109, 114, 121, 173, 192
representation metrics 203
resistors 224
respect 79, 135
restructuring 67–68, 69–70
retention metrics 203
return on investment (ROI) 199–203
reward 130, 171–93
    see also base pay (salary); benefits package; bonuses (incentive plans); cash (money); compensation; perks
role definition 56–59, 73, 116, 159–60
role/person misalignment 69

salaries 172, 175, 176, 183, 191
salary reviews 176
Sales function 68–69, 72, 174, 183
scalability 6, 53, 120
selection metrics 203
self-audits 37, 97
self-awareness 14, 32–40, 42, 46, 48–49, 93, 153, 158, 205–06, 212
self-reflection 30, 37
separation (leaving organizations) 119, 131, 148–49, 199, 203
    see also exit interviews
servant leadership 101
7-S Model 222–23
shared purpose 31
short-term focus 68–69, 187
significant organizational tensions 71–72
simplicity 81, 207
skills 57–59, 101–23, 159–62
    see also specialization (specific skills)
skills assessment 115–16, 117–18
skills updates 117
sleep test 37

small gestures 187
social intelligence 108, 114
    see also self-awareness
social media 119, 200
    see also Facebook; Glassdoor
soft (social) skills 58, 114, 118, 121–22
solution-finding 160
sourcing see talent sourcing (hiring)
spans of control 54, 72, 110
specialization (specific skills) 55, 60, 62, 111
specific skills requirements 111
specificity 28
stakeholders 23, 25, 104, 133, 201, 223, 224
    reward design 187, 190, 197, 199
Starbucks 84
start-ups 16, 43, 53, 54–55, 111, 113, 141, 175, 180, 181–82
state of flow 163, 167, 168
'stickiness' 44–45
strategy 30, 155
    business 27, 57, 68, 71, 112, 114, 117, 182–83
    environmental 184, 185
    philanthropic 185, 186
strengths 32, 33, 115
surveys 153–54
    core values 80–82
    customer 200
    engagement 149–53, 164, 166–67, 200, 204, 220
Sustainable Living (Unilever) 185
swim lane diagrams 73

Talent Acquisition teams 131
talent sourcing (hiring) 56–67, 70, 91–92, 112, 125–46, 219–20
    non-traditional 209
    see also gig economy (workers); interviews; recruitment
talent sourcing (hiring) assessment 70, 219–20
tangible rewards 183
targets, DI&B 197
task management 60
team dynamics 13, 15–17, 24, 38, 61–64, 155
team dynamics assessment 15–17, 155
team managers (leaders) 60, 98
team size 72
teams 52–53, 72
    consultation with 38, 40, 78
    core values design 78–79, 80, 82, 88, 129
    EVP design 129–30, 131
    see also expert teams; guiding teams; team dynamics; team managers (leaders)
tech savviness (technical skills) 104, 112, 121–22
technical values 83
technology 120–21
tensions 16–17, 42, 46, 65, 69, 71–72, 95
testing 106, 132
themes 23, 47, 80, 82, 83, 112, 131
TIAA 205
time management 13
tolerating behaviour 38
total rewards (TR) 171–93
    see also base pay (salary); benefits package; bonuses (incentive plans); career development; cash (money); compensation; leadership development (management development); perks; recognition; well-being
total rewards assessment 188–89, 220
total rewards inventory 189
total rewards philosophy 175
total rewards plans 189–90
total rewards statements 188
town hall (all-employee) meetings 79, 80, 85, 108, 158
toxic culture 38–40, 44, 98, 173
training 43, 114, 201–02, 203
transactional reward programmes 188
Transition Model 223
transparency 107, 156, 157, 201
trickle-down effect 65, 94, 149
trust 31, 40, 61, 134, 147–49, 157, 160, 164–65

underperformance 16, 110, 165
    see also low performers
Unilever 128, 132, 184–85
urgency 93, 223

value propositions
    customer 127–28
    EVP 127–35, 140, 142–44, 145–46, 204, 219–20
values 11–12, 29, 41, 75–100, 137–39, 178
    core 17–18, 31, 36, 65, 174–75, 180–82, 222
    leadership 13–14
    see also beliefs; value propositions
values alignment (misalignment) 41, 86–87, 93–94, 97, 139

values definition 83–85
values fit 137–39
values interviews 138–39
values review 87
variable pay 172, 183
visibility 41, 42, 93, 164, 198
vision 6, 21, 43, 75, 185, 224
volunteerism *185*, 186
vulnerability 21, 205

war on talent 125–26, 175
weaknesses 32, 33, 34
well-being 32, 40, 173, 175, 180, 186, 206
White Privilege 211–12
work environment 7, 130, 206
work ethic 120, 137
work-life balance 4–5, 148

Zappos 135–36

CPSIA information can be obtained
at www.ICGtesting.com
Printed in the USA
BVHW020957190221
600307BV00007B/2